A WOR DIFFEI
THE BiG GREEN POETRY MACHINE

Recycle, Recycle, Recycle! Love the world you live in. Be good to your planet. Don't be mean, be green! Recycle, Recycle! Love the world you live in. Be good to your planet. Don't be mean, be green! Recycle, Recycle, Recycle! Love the world

Southern Verses

Edited by Helen Davies

First published in Great Britain in 2009 by:

 Young**Writers**

Young Writers
Remus House
Coltsfoot Drive
Peterborough
PE2 9JX
Telephone: 01733 890066
Website: www.youngwriters.co.uk

Foreword

Young Writers' A World of Difference is a showcase for our nation's most brilliant young poets to share their thoughts, hopes and fears for the planet they call home.

Young Writers was established in 1990 to nurture creativity in our children and young adults, to give them an interest in poetry and an outlet to express themselves. Seeing their work in print will encourage them to keep writing as they grow, and become our poets of tomorrow.

Selecting the poems has been challenging and immensely rewarding. The effort and imagination invested by these young writers makes their poems a pleasure to enjoy reading time and time again.

Contents

Astor College for the Arts, Dover

The Poems

War!

War is bad,
War is sad,
So bring back our soldiers,
They're not built like boulders.

War is not a game,
It won't bring you to fame,
It only brings pain,
Get that in your brain.

I am a soldier writing to you,
Because I have no clue what to do,
I've changed my mind about the war,
I don't feel like fighting anymore,
I have no idea why I came,
All I feel now is just shame.

I am on the battlefield,
Cold and alone,
All I want to do is go home,
I can't imagine the pain,
My family will go through,
If they get the letter,
That says I won't be coming home to you.

All I need is to find a way,
That I can hide,
So that I can live at least one more day.

I'm on the battlefield,
It starts to rain,
Bang! Bang! I'm dead,
Oh no, the shame.

Michelle Aloe & Adam Robert Arthur (12)
Astor College for the Arts, Dover

What You're Doing To The Earth

Think of our Earth as our body,
It feels, it hurts and gets infected,
This happens to anybody,
It's like a drug that's being injected.

People who litter,
Are just careless and bitter,
This has a big effect on us,
So stop making a fuss.

This world could be a better place.

With breathable air,
Cleaner water,
With people who care.

Believe it or not, people can die
And become seriously ill.

This isn't a lie,
Pollution can be poisonous gases,
Not good for our lungs,
Which can make us choke and lose our tongues.

So take care,
When walking into air
And maybe you could help the Earth to heal,
By simply recycling an old tyre wheel.

Louise Hall (13)
Astor College for the Arts, Dover

Endangered Animals

There once were two cheetahs, two creatures and two cages,
The cheetahs and the creatures lived in the two cages at the zoo,
They all wished they were all back in the wild,
Away from this horrible zoo.

When will it ever stop?
Time after time, one by one,
We lose another and never to be seen again.

Amy Pilcher (11)
Astor College for the Arts, Dover

Pollution

There is a lot of pollution,
But there's always a solution,
You could recycle,
Or ride on your bicycle.

There are many ways to save the world.

Jump on a double-decker bus,
It saves a lot of fuss,
Don't waste gas,
Don't follow the mass.

There are many ways to save the world.

Don't have baths,
Don't be daft,
Have a shower,
You'll feel like a flower.

There are many ways to save the world.

Don't chop down trees,
You won't have a breeze,
You'll feel so refreshed,
That you're doing your best.

There are many ways to save the world.

Sophie-Ann Bullock (11)
Astor College for the Arts, Dover

What's In The War?

Devastation as families are broken up,
Blood, sweat and tears fill the atmosphere,
Dead bodies everywhere, because they can't sort our their problems,
Some are saved but others aren't,
Innocent murders as we speak,
Guns, grenades and bombs awaiting to attack,
People in the same country fighting against each other,
Hospitals are overflowing,
Fires and suicides all around.

Taneka Walford & Sinead Driver (13)
Astor College for the Arts, Dover

3

For My Country

The building stood as still as a pebble,
As silent as a deserted prison,
I remember when I was playing with my friends,
But it's interrupted by the piercing sound of glass hitting the ground,
The dust falls from ceilings as the tank patrols the city,
I hear them searching the houses and buildings,
Luckily I'm safe because I have an attic,
A hidden one,
Even though I'm safe, I just wish they'd go,
The high-pitched squeal of the jets circling the area,
The dust fills the air as the helicopter lands,
I can't help but to think what's going to happen next?
The thumping of my heart sounds like a Titan stomping,
Adrenaline fills my body,
I start to shake like mad!
I hear the footsteps hitting the floorboards,
Bam!
It all stops,
Adrenaline rushes out of my body leaving me powerless,
I'm cold and scared,
But I must stay strong, for my family, for my friends,
For my country!

Xavier Lavocat (13)
Astor College for the Arts, Dover

Going, Going, Gone!

There once was a dolphin called Dan,
Twenty one snakes who lived in a van,
A lemur and a hippo,
A giraffe called Kippo
And a polar bear, who's becoming quite rare.

The bear locked up in chains
And the tigers who live near the cranes,
They're all slowly dying,
Now the people are crying,
It's time to start showing we care.

Daniel Christopher Parkes (12)
Astor College for the Arts, Dover

We're In Trouble!

The world's in trouble,
So are we,
We kill the plants
And all the trees.

War kills people
And the Earth,
Guns, swords and bombs,
Babies killed at birth.

Litter is everywhere,
Created by Man,
Put your rubbish in the bin
And be nature's number one fan.

Pollution is bad,
It damages land and sea,
Fumes from a car,
Affecting you and me.

If we just recycle,
To help the human race,
Cans, paper and plastic,
The world's a better place.

Annalee Austin (14)
Astor College for the Arts, Dover

World Peace

People want world peace, stop all the war,
People don't want war in the world anymore,
Think of the family, think of the Earth,
Think of the children, waiting for birth,
Stop all the shooting, stop all the killing,
To stop this, you need to be willing,
Make the world a nicer place,
We're all the same human race,
Why can't we just get along?
Why can't we have world peace?

Harrison O'Brien (13)
Astor College for the Arts, Dover

Rainforest

Why can't we be green?
Why can't we recycle?
All we are doing is destroying our lives,
Destroying the Earth.

Animals are becoming extinct,
They are losing their homes,
Destroying the rainforests can destroy humans' homes,
As floods will be coming down the hill faster,
As there is not going to any trees to slow the water.

Lakes are getting polluted,
Killing all the fish,
Rainforests are going to look ugly,
If we keep destroying all the rainforests in the world,
Trees provide us with oxygen,
So we could be losing oxygen.

Rainforests grow fruit,
They also grow cocoa,
So if we kill the rainforest,
We wouldn't be able to have all of these,
We need fruit to survive!

Hannah Johnson & Fern Parker (13)
Astor College for the Arts, Dover

Trees Need Us

God made bees,
Bees made honey,
Trees were chopped
And people made a lot of money.
Leaves fall down into mud,
Trees go down with a big thud.
Wood is collected,
Wood is sold,
Wood is made into a mould
And as the trees are lost,
The world grows old.

Katie Hodge & Paige Kinch (13)
Astor College for the Arts, Dover

War Is A Waste

Some people fight for religion,
Some people fight for power,
But it does not matter,
Because war is a waste of time.

Bombs go boom,
Then they go bang
And then the leader said, 'Soon they'll be dead.'

My friend is dying,
My other is dead,
I cry with mercy,
And say . . .

'War is a waste,
Why am I in this place?
I must get my friend into a bed,
And save him from being shot in the head.'

So I say try not to fight,
Just come to a conclusion,
Do not fight, do not fight
And have a good life.

Ben Smith (13)
Astor College for the Arts, Dover

Homeless People

Tramps on the street,
Showing their smelly feet,
Getting cold, growing mould,
Asking for spare change,
Wishing they could change,
The dogs are starving,
People are laughing,
Sleeps at night in a cardboard box,
People look at him throwing rocks,
He walks around the town in the middle of the night,
Teenagers asking for a fight.

Andrw Crush (13)
Astor College for the Arts, Dover

Endangered Animals

Cars pollute the air, so we are killing all the bears,
Tigers are big now, they have to dig because they are dying.

The sea is rough, the fishing nets are out,
The dolphins are getting trapped and they cannot get out.

The turtles are small, they are swimming round and round,
There is not so many of them that can be found.

The sea is rising, whales are dying,
Now there is not so many birds flying.

White rhinos are charging across the African plain,
Killing them must be insane.

Elephants are killed for their ivory tusks,
Because some men think they're an absolute must.

Cheetahs run for freedom and fun,
They must hurry to avoid the bullet from the gun.

Panda's chew bamboo then rest,
Because they think they are the best.

Becky Baker (11)
Astor College for the Arts, Dover

Pollution

Pollution stop it,
Catch the bus to school, it's cool,
So stop pollution.

Pollution smells bad,
Close down the power stations,
Save the world and now!

Pollution, stop it,
Don't throw toxins in water,
So stop pollution.

Pollution smells bad,
So stop having bonfires,
So save the world and now!

Jasmine Swan (12)
Astor College for the Arts, Dover

War

Guns firing in to the darkness,
Hearing children falling,
See children dying.

Building echoing from gunfire,
Never-ending,
Never fading.

People hiding in corners of houses and buildings,
Wishing they were somewhere else
And suddenly when they think it's all over,
They are gone from this world.

And after the fighting there is nothing,
No happiness,
No joy,
Just sorrow.

And the crying of people that have lost loved ones,
And the silence of entire cities,
And over entire oceans.

Peter Knight (13)
Astor College for the Arts, Dover

Endangered Animals

The sea is rough,
The fishing nets are out,
The dolphins are getting trapped
And they cannot get out.
Cars pollute the air,
So we are killing all the bears,
Tigers are big, now people have to dig,
Because they are dying,
Foxes are crawling,
Because they keep falling,
Turtles are slow
And they don't grow.

Because they are all dying.

Sophie De-La-Mere (11)
Astor College for the Arts, Dover

I Write About . . .

I write about a war,
A war that never ends,
A war that never stops,
A war, war which no one stops.

I write about guns,
Guns which demolish,
Guns who kill,
Guns which make us miserable.

I write about people,
People who sacrifice,
Sacrifice their lives,
Lives they had once.

Bombs what about them?
They just say one word,
Boom!
And we are all gone.

Ignas Dilevicius (13)
Astor College for the Arts, Dover

War

The war has come,
Fighting, anger,
Not knowing what is happening,
I am scared, I don't know what I am doing.

War, war,
Bad, bad war,
Why all the fighting?
Like hunters on a killing spree,
The war has come,
Smoke, explosion,
I have had no rest in days,
I don't know what I'm doing here.

Help,
Or I am going to die.

Emma Cook (12)
Astor College for the Arts, Dover

10

The Trooper

There he stands firm and still,
Rifle on arm, ready to kill,
His shining boots fastened up tight,
A few more minutes till the last big fight.

The gunshots echo inside his head,
His back still aching from his bare wooden bed,
No birds in this desert, merrily singing,
Their triggers pinging and pinging.

Fall to the floor to take cover,
In his mind a picture of his lover,
Why can't these wars just end?
His friends, the wounded not on the mend.

War is blood spilt for no reason,
Another on the way for next season,
Why can't our world just get along?
In this world does peace belong?

Katie Ashton (13)
Astor College for the Arts, Dover

Smile Or Frown?

Sizzle, burn and crippled away,
It could be happy and fun,
For people to play,
Or it could be miserable, unhappy,
Where no one can play,
Where everyone is unhappy,
And there's no lights,
Where everyone is happy,
And the sun shines bright,
The drill in your ear,
Or the smile on your face,
Which one will it be?
A smile or a frown!
You decide.

Emily-Anne Nelmes (12)
Astor College for the Arts, Dover

Did You Know?

A packet of crisps fell to the ground,
But the boy that dropped them didn't make a sound!
I told the boy to pick up the litter,
He looked at me and said, 'See ya!'

Did you know the world could end?
Did you know you're not setting a trend?
Did you know animals are dying?
Because of your crisps on the ground lying!

Your littering is killing the Earth,
Did you know what it is worth?

The boy walked off and I was sad,
I guess my facts were really bad!
All of a sudden, the boy came up,
Picked up his litter with a grump!
Maybe I did make a difference,
I'm glad someone took the time to listen!

Laura Johnson & Chanelle King (12)
Astor College for the Arts, Dover

Why Go To War?

I'm in the army, so I have to go to war
And if I didn't I would break the law,
Fighting, suffering, crashing down,
'Help over here, there's a man down,'
Damp green mould in my tent,
Sun goes down and then it went,
Crashing, thumping in my sleep,
Death and sadness makes me weep,
Loss of friends brings pain to my heart,
Going outside looks like death depart,
War is a terrible place to be,
But they can see,
A nightmarish look in your eyes,
And bang, you'll have a sad surprise.

Drew Burrett (13)
Astor College for the Arts, Dover

Life Is Lost

Bang!
I smell the gunpowder lingering in the air,
The smell of people dying,
The smell of death,
Screams and blood, the silence,
A baby crying in the arms of her dead mother.

Bang!
Complete silence,
There is nothing left,
Life is lost and dead,
Even the youngest life is gone,
Why is this? Why?
Blood and violence,
Families destroyed for nothing,
They never deserved to die,
It needs to stop!

Ella Skinner (13)
Astor College for the Arts, Dover

Recycling

Don't put your rubbish on the floor,
Put it in a box outside your front door,
Recycling people will come and take it away,
And make it into something new that day.
Recycling includes glass, plastic, clothes and tins,
So don't forget to put your rubbish in recycling bins.
Don't waste paper and save the trees,
Just pick up your box, it's not much to ease,
Recycling means reduce and reuse,
So pick up and recycle your bottle of booze,
You can recycle metal by melting it down,
Then make it into something that could be brown,
So reduce, reuse, recycle, it's really easy,
It's really fun too and won't make you queasy.

Finlay Storey (12)
Astor College for the Arts, Dover

Endangered Animals

Our beautiful wild animals
Are slowly dying,
Because we do not care,
People have stopped trying
To help save lions, tigers and bears.

If we don't help now,
They will become so rare.

Driving around in our cars
Is making pollution in the air,
It's killing the wildlife around our home,
Please think about it and take care,
Because badgers and foxes are dying
From cars and hunters too.

We need to help them to stay alive,
Your choice, it's up to you!

Emma Hadley (11)
Astor College for the Arts, Dover

War!

War is a verdict,
War is a pain,
All the guns,
All every day.

The soldiers that cry,
The destruction that thrives,
How will they survive
In this cruel world?
They will die.

If we stopped,
It would be grand,
It's a happy world,
Forever to last.

Brandon Cameron (10)
Astor College for the Arts, Dover

War

War is scary,
Death and wounds,
Why can't we stop?
Why can't we have peace?
Bombs, explosions,
Why can't we stop?
Why can't we have peace?
Scars, bruises,
Why can't we stop?
Why can't we have peace?
Sad families, sad friends,
Why can't we stop?
Why can't we have *peace?*

Georgia Sophia Holmes (13)
Astor College for the Arts, Dover

Tell Someone!

Doesn't matter the colour of your skin,
When there's a bully nobody wins,
It goes from the kids inside school,
To the teens in university halls,
If you're being bullied, remember to *shout,*
Don't think there's any way out,
If you're standing there watching a fight,
You're just as bad, and it's not right,
You're holding families in suspense,
Just for your fun and your expense,
If you're a bully reading this rhyme,
We hope you stop bullying because
It's a crime!

Robyn Bunyard & Nasebar Miah (12)
Astor College for the Arts, Dover

Homeless

I sit here on my own,
With no money and no home,
I have no family, no friends,
I am all alone,
I cry myself to sleep,
While stared at on the street,
I don't know why I deserve this,
I've never had a hug,
I've never had a kiss,
I have no one to hold,
In this freezing cold,
I play music to earn money,
People don't care, they just think it's funny.

Daniel Ellis & Rebecca Dowle (12)
Astor College for the Arts, Dover

Recycle

My poem is about recycling stuff,
With everyone's help it might be enough,
If people recycle paper and shoes,
There's a good chance we cannot lose.

If people collect bottles and tins
And use their recycle bins,
In our campaign there will be highs and lows,
But in our world that's just how it goes.

Litter and trash is all we see,
Picking it up is the key,
So do it today and don't delay,
Recycling trash is the only way.

Jack Tong (12)
Astor College for the Arts, Dover

Poem Planet

War is for wild boar,
But pollution is
Not the solution.

And save the animals in the trees,
For our lovely bumblebees,
On the other hand . . .
Extinction is not the
Proper reaction,
So . . .
Start working and
Stop smoking,
And save our planet.

Billy Perkins & Reece Jaconelli (12)
Astor College for the Arts, Dover

War

War sucks, war is bad,
It kills mankind wherever it goes,
It makes the world sad in every part of it.

War sucks, war is bad,
It hurts everyone even if you're not in it,
It hurts, it's not cool and most people die from it.

War is the worst, everyone hates it,
It destroys everything in its path
And some wars, terrorists start, it's rubbish.

In one war, over 100,000 soldiers died in the first hour,
I bet we all wish that war wasn't real.

Fraser Shields & Ashley Wright (12)
Astor College for the Arts, Dover

War

I crawl to the ground, hurt in my mouth,
I am slow and as quiet as a mouse,
My fellow soldiers are shot to the ground,
As I walk through the streets,
I see plenty of dead feet,
As we go in to war our troops are hurt more,
I see a child in despair and I go and look for more anywhere,
We see the enemy, now it's time to get ready,
We wait, we wait, we just wait,
We've come home now, it's a relief to hear no sound,
So that's the end of the war, I don't want to do it anymore,
If we go back, I don't know if I'll come back.

Alex Dyer (13)
Astor College for the Arts, Dover

The World

If the world was deserted with no trees,
We wouldn't want to live here,
If the world was trapped with heat because of pollution,
We wouldn't want to live here,
If the world had non-stop war going on,
We wouldn't want to live here,
Some things we need to stop,
Some things we shouldn't have even started,
The world is like a delicate piece of glass,
It can only take so much pressure,
If the world had all these going on,
We wouldn't live, and we couldn't live here.

Bethany Ward (12)
Astor College for the Arts, Dover

Rainforests

Where are all the rainforests going?
Are they being cut down for paper we use today?
Are they being cut down for houses?
What we do not realise is that we are killing all
The little insects and animals that hibernate or live there,
Think of all the tigers, leopards and orangu-tans that have lost
Their lives, their homes and their food to help them live,
I think we should put a stop to the rainforests
That are being cut down,
It is our fault that the animals like
Tigers, leopards and orangu-tans are becoming
More and more extinct.

Shantell Banks (14)
Astor College for the Arts, Dover

The Power

The beating drums deep inside you,
The flashes of burning rays,
Carry through the wind,
The bleeding souls of those who are lost, linger.

The dark streets are flooded,
With tears that have fallen from the broken
And the pain that has been drained from the injured.

The deep stench of heartache,
Still remains in the gut-wrenched battlefields that were once
Filled with life,
This is the power of war!

Coutney Wain (14) & Abbey McCluskey (13)
Astor College for the Arts, Dover

Save The World

We live in a world of pollution,
But what it really is, is execution.

We throw away things broken without a thought,
Even if it was last year, it was bought.

Don't let people harm the world,
Preserve and recycle, stand out from the crowd.

If just one person extra from every town acted wisely,
There would be no need to frown.

So come on everybody and do the right thing,
Protect the world and stop it ending.

Lauren Killen (13)
Astor College for the Arts, Dover

What I Want To See

The animals run in fear,
The bush fire is getting near,
A zebra is running the opposite way,
He doesn't know it's his last day,
A net is hiding up a tree,
So high up, he couldn't see,
This was such a brutal killing,
The zebra will now be sold for a shilling,
Letting the animals roam free,
How wonderful this would be,
Because this is what I want to see.

Sophie Weymouth (13)
Astor College for the Arts, Dover

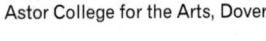

The Frontlines

We lie here quietly, as still as the night air,
We had nothing to do but to stare,
To be fair, we didn't have time to spare,
Until the time came, we thought this was all a game,
But if we get back, we don't want the fame,
Or if not we might die in vain,
We didn't move until the tanks came,
And then the time came and we ran,
Into the frontline,
The fields of war!

Dominic Button (14)
Astor College for the Arts, Dover

Child Abuse!

Sad, lonely, a child abused,
Feels worried, alone and confused,
Even though the abuser could face jail,
They still make the child whine and wail.
Alone and unhappy, the child walks in fear,
Even if they cry, no one wants to hear,
All worried, sad, alone,
A small child won't go home,
Child abuse, it's not a nice thing, it's all hate,
Stop it now before it's too late . . .

Laura Palmer & Emma Pearce (12)
Astor College for the Arts, Dover

Homeless People

Nearly every day there is someone new living on the streets,
These sorts of people look like strange freaks,
They are smelly, sweaty, old, dirty, strange and weird,
All these people need beds, baths to clean in, food, water and love,
Open more hostels and you can help prevent this!

Danielle Burns (13)
Astor College for the Arts, Dover

Modern Warfare

October 2008, Afghanistan,
It is blazing hot and I am sat in the long grass
With all my equipment and mainly my guns,
My M40, A3, M15, a few grenades, and a
RD6 waiting for a sudden movement in the distance.
Bang! I can hear down the mike.
'Is everything OK John?' I bellowed
'I'm fine mate, there are Taliban around,' he whispers.
This is when my heart cries out for my family
But I can't go home now, so I stay put as I was commanded.

Joe Morrison
Astor College for the Arts, Dover

Worst Enemy

Pollution is the world's worst enemy,
It makes the sky so poor,
Coal is its best friend,
Fuel is also a friend,
Bonfires, fires and BBQs make the sky dark,
Rubbish and landfill sites mixed together,
Make them overload,
So you must recycle,
Recycle,
Recycle.

Atalanta Tolputt (12)
Astor College for the Arts, Dover

War

War is bad, shooting and fighting,
Booting and hooting,
Guns and bombs,
It's so bad and grand,
It's so bad!

Thomas Wallis (12)
Astor College for the Arts, Dover

Recycling

Don't cut down the trees,
Cos there won't be any habitat for the bees.
Use more recycle bins,
Where you can put your cans and tins.
Remember don't waste paper,
Just use it for later.
Don't let your water spill,
Cos then you will get a big water bill.
Recycling is cool,
You should do it everywhere, even at school.

Kayleigh Payne & Chloe Larman (12)
Astor College for the Arts, Dover

Loss Of Trees

When trees are cut down,
More sick people can be lost,
People are dying.

Where is everyone?
More people have really died,
What is the result?

Stop destroying trees,
Stop chopping down all the trees,
Stop taking forests.

Shannon Knott (12)
Astor College for the Arts, Dover

War!

Terrorists come from Afghanistan,
With their nuclear bombs and air strikes
And we blow them up with our tanks,
Now take a terrorist's gun and get two roses,
Put them together and you get guns and roses.

Alex Hawes & Brandon Faulkner (12)
Astor College for the Arts, Dover

The World Is Crying Out For Help

P ollution is all around us,
O n and off the back end of a bus,
L itter is everywhere, it smells and it stinks,
L oss of trees means less of the minks,
U nborn babies at the risk of dying,
T rust never around, people always lying,
I ce caps melting, sea levels rising,
O bese people trying to lose pounds by exercising,
N ever-ending words to describe the pain the world is in.

Katie Prior (13)
Astor College for the Arts, Dover

War!

War is loud, painful and horrible,
You can hear bullets flying through the air,
Boats sinking, planes crashing,
People dying,
Why do people start war?
Hatred, evilness, revenge or just for fun?
This is war,
Get used to it or you're going to die.
War!

Thaddeus Wilson (11)
Astor College for the Arts, Dover

War!

War is bad,
All it does is make people sad,
Wars come and go every year,
Don't shoot the enemy in the eye,
Because no one really deserves to die,
So don't let off your atomic bomb,
Cos one big bang and everyone's gone.

Jacob Sheppard (12) & Daniel Tucker (13)
Astor College for the Arts, Dover

Recycle, Recycle

Recycle, recycle,
All you can,
Then you'll see the world again,
We will see how it goes,
All the highs and lows,
Mum said, 'Go recycle tins,
Instead of using bins.'
Dad said, 'Go recycle oil,
Instead of catching a boil.'

Lewis Allison (12)
Astor College for the Arts, Dover

Pollution

P ollution could involve the police,
O ceans are polluted,
L itter is pollution,
L akes are polluted,
U sing bins people do not,
T V is electricity pollution,
I dea - people have no idea what bad pollution is,
O zone layer protects the Earth,
N aughty people pollute the Earth.

Olivia Smith (12)
Astor College for the Arts, Dover

Why War?

War is dramatic, no need to fight,
Poor people are always sacrificed,
No more, no war, that's what we need,
Bleed, bleed, it is always that way, why oh why?
Guns vibrating, war is not the law,
I can hear the bombs, don't do any wrongs,
War is not the law.

Kieron Pilcher (13)
Astor College for the Arts, Dover

Is It Worth It?

Countries fighting, a horrible sighting,
Tanks are coming, people are running,
Knocking down doors, bullet shells on floors,
Guns are blazing, pressure raising,
Bullets flying, people dying,
People bloody, cold and muddy,
Gasps for breath, sound of death,
After the kill, nothing but still,
Peace for a bit, is it worth it?

Morgan Weakley (12)
Astor College for the Arts, Dover

World At War

When World War One started,
The kids were sent away to another place,
But why should this happen?
They should stay with their mothers,
But why can't they?
Because the bombs can kill,
World wars, why should it kill?
Why should we have it?
Who knows!

Danielle Blythe (11)
Astor College for the Arts, Dover

The War

There is a war, there is a war,
They're fighting for the poor, the poor,
The houses are falling, falling to the ground,
Crash, bang wallop!
The bombs are here! Let's get in the bomb shelter,
And cry a tear!
Let's sing! Let's cheer! The war is over!

Abigail Willcox (11)
Astor College for the Arts, Dover

This Is Peace

Peace, the sound of children's laughter as joy and happiness,
Comes to end the pain and sadness,
Peace, the end of all wars,
The time to rebuild, as rainbow colours flood the land no more,
Blood to be spilt,
Peace, the wiping of the tears,
A hug of a loved one,
Time to dance and smile is for all,
As this is peace.

James Booth (13)
Astor College for the Arts, Dover

War

Bombs going off in the street,
Gunfire everywhere you see,
Soldiers running on their feet,
As people die in the street,
The car explodes,
As women scream!
When silence strikes in the street,
Corpses everywhere you see,
Children crying while adults peer into the street.

Dale Miller (13)
Astor College for the Arts, Dover

War

Screams, *bang, bang, bang!*
You can hear the tanks rolling.
The guns on the tank
Sound like elephants' footsteps.
The battleships crash against the waves,
Bombs sound like rocks
Tumbling down from the clifftops.

Jamie Glover (11)
Astor College for the Arts, Dover

War

War is a bad thing,
It can cause loads of deaths,
More and more people go out there,
Then they are dying,
Then less come back and the families are crying,
There's loads of bombs and explosions,
Then innocent people die,
The more and more terrorists there are,
The more dead people lie.

Rhys McNeill & William M-Woad (13)
Astor College for the Arts, Dover

War

When you're out on the battlefield,
Dust and dirt is flying,
My friend has just been killed,
All my friends keep dying.

When you're sitting in a tank,
What if you had C4 stuck to your head?
Will you still be sitting comfortably,
Even when you're dead?

Rhys McGarry (13)
Astor College for the Arts, Dover

The Never-Ending War

Crash! Bang! Boom!
I hear it again, everything goes silent,
The guns, the bombs, they're all so violent,
Soldiers injured and soldiers dying,
Families scared, screaming and crying,
Will this madness ever end?

Jessica Elizabeth Clark (13)
Astor College for the Arts, Dover

Reduce, Reuse, Recycle, Recycle Now!

Reduce, reuse, recycle,
Remember the R's,
Reduce, reuse, recycle,
Always do those things.

Recycle now!
Recycle paper,
Bottles, cans, plastic and glass,
Recycle old clothes.

Frankie George (12)
Astor College for the Arts, Dover

Credit Crunch

It's the credit crunch,
It's like a violent punch,
Your money will be less,
So, your life becomes a mess.

Everyone is becoming poor,
Because the government want more,
So, it's the credit crunch,
It's like a violent punch.

Kayleigh Biggs (12)
Astor College for the Arts, Dover

Electricity

To save electricity,
All you have to do
Is turn off a light switch,
When it's not being used,
To save your money
And the Earth,
Don't waste electricity,
For all it's worth . . .

Nikita Lawrence (12)
Astor College for the Arts, Dover

Poor People

Poor people grow their food,
They're never in the party mood,
It's cold at night,
They have to fight for their own rights,
They have no money
And I'm not being funny,
Poor people work all day and don't rest,
The work they do is a pest.

Emily Jayne Husk (12)
Astor College for the Arts, Dover

The War

There's no need to start a war,
Just because a country's poor,
I see dead people on the floor,
This shouldn't happen anymore,
My head is sore,
They broke the law,
I can't sit through this anymore,
I will help us win the war.

Abigayle Howbrook (13)
Astor College for the Arts, Dover

The Almighty Rainforest

As its height is now dwindling to a bush in a garden,
With its great animals, big and small,
Lies the jaguar to an ant, from a tapir to a frog,
They are almighty and free, yet we are losing them,
Tree to tree is falling every day,
Cattle ranches are being built to feed us,
Yet all animals around the world are
Pleading for their survival!

Stanley Hall (12)
Astor College for the Arts, Dover

War - When Will It Stop?

Our people are dying every day,
Still, not moving as they lay,
Blood, blood everywhere,
Ours and the enemies that we share,
When, when will it end
And turn the enemy into a friend?
The noise of the bombs coming down,
The only thing to do is close your eyes and frown.

Jake James Ward (13)
Astor College for the Arts, Dover

Recycle

It cleans up the Earth,
So we can see the turf,
If you recycle bottles, paper and cans,
You will get back the land,
You can help stop pollution,
With this solution,
So save the world
And make it twirl.

Tessa Williams (13)
Astor College for the Arts, Dover

Pollution

Gases and smoke are horrible things,
I say to people you know there are bins,
A very old lady known as a knitter,
Is so much better than chewing gum and litter,
Using too much electricity is bad,
It makes me so very, very mad,
It makes the world so very dark,
All you can hear is dogs bark, bark, bark.

Alfie Pye (12)
Astor College for the Arts, Dover

Trees, Trees, Lovely Trees

Trees, trees, lovely trees,
They are everywhere,
Care for them,
They may make lots of lovely stuff,
But we need them more than anything,
So please, please care for them,
Trees, trees, lovely trees,
Swaying in the breeze.

Jade Mincher & Paige Burrett (12)
Astor College for the Arts, Dover

The War

This war is making me miserable,
Because of people dying,
Guns and tanks are coming
And I am running,
All I see is darkness and no people there,
I see my friend's body and hope he rests peacefully there.

Declan Tobin & Cully Riley (12)
Astor College for the Arts, Dover

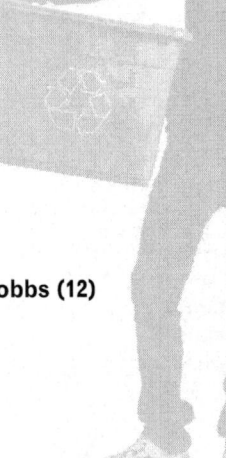

Bored!

I'm sitting out here,
On the dirty, wet, hard floor,
I have no money,
People find it quite funny,
Please help us dear Lord,
I am extremely bored!

Charlotte McColvin & Karla Hobbs (12)
Astor College for the Arts, Dover

War

War is bad,
War is sad.
The sound of the bangs and crashes,
The soldiers crying from cuts and slashes,
If war was no more,
No one would be homeless or poor.

Bradley Wilkins (12)
Astor College for the Arts, Dover

War!

War! War! What is war?
Death's open door,
Soldiers fight for lives and their pride,
Whilst we are safe on the other side,
So don't take things for granted,
Because our soldiers have fought.

Shay Brock-Carey (12)
Astor College for the Arts, Dover

Rainforest Sights

Orange, green, pink and red,
All these colours in my head,
Bark, soil, life and leaves,
Animals playing in the trees,
Rustle, trickle, flutter and call,
In the rainforest, I feel so small.

Emily Edwards Little (13)
Astor College for the Arts, Dover

Why Do We Go To War?

Waking up to burning,
Thought everyone was learning,
All I saw was dead people,
That must mean the guns are lethal!

Why do we go to war?

Kyla Walker (13)
Astor College for the Arts, Dover

Global Warming

God was sitting in bed,
Global warming hit him on the head,
God tied up his lace,
Punched it in the face,
Now global warming is dead.

Thomas Trethewey-Williams (13)
Astor College for the Arts, Dover

War Zone

War is bad,
War is sad,
Aeroplanes fly
And people die,
All the people want to cry.

Jack Fagg, Jordan Caldwell & Cameron McHugh (13)
Astor College for the Arts, Dover

34

Pollution

Pollution, stop burning fires,
Pollution, stop it and save the world,
Pollution, stop it before it's too late.

Ashley Swinerd (13)
Astor College for the Arts, Dover

Crash! - Haiku

Crash! The sound of trees,
Animals in a riot,
Oxygen dying.

Cameron Keyes & Mark Sansam (13)
Astor College for the Arts, Dover

Extinction - Haiku

Some animals die,
Some animals are extinct,
Let's help them to live.

Rebecca Gliddon & Barnabus Rollings-Mathews (13)
Astor College for the Arts, Dover

Saving The Planet

We're always told to turn the light off,
When we leave the room,
To always turn the tap off,
When we're cleaning our teeth too,
Never to leave things on standby,
Turn off at the plug,
To have a shower, not a bath,
To give our world a hug.

Aletia Neilly (12)
Dartford Grammar School for Girls, Dartford

If Only

If only there was a machine,
To tell us wrong from right,
Someone to pick up the pieces,
Of the next gang fight.

In a flash, a life is taken,
In one moment, a tree's cut down,
In a second, a war has started,
One less girl in a bridal gown.

We take basic things for granted,
Shelter, water, warmth and food,
Soon we'll use up all resources,
Fuels which cannot be renewed.

This could be prevented,
We could say 'No more,'
To the hurt and suffering,
Of poverty and war.

If only there was a way to
Go back and change the past,
Create a better future,
A world that will last.

Some people do not realise,
The impact of their choices,
They should not go ahead and act,
Not listen to others' voices.

If only there was a machine,
To tell us wrong from right,
The world would be a better place,
With the future in our sight.

Layla Kimberley Parvez (13)
Dartford Grammar School for Girls, Dartford

Don't Bake!

The world is getting warmer than tea in a cup,
Before long we'll all burn up,
The ozone layer is melting away,
It won't come back when we want to play.

Is there a red light on your TV?
No, hooray, well done, whoopee,
Yes, oh no, that's extremely bad,
Turn it off at the wall, make the world glad.

Greenhouse gases are reduced by trees,
Don't cut them down, plant more please,
Old trees for paper, they don't work as well,
Plant new ones where the others fell.

It costs the environment to make water pure,
Leaving your tap on is no cure,
Turn off the tap when cleaning your teeth,
Australia needs water in the Great Barrier Reef.

Get on a bus instead of a car,
Reduce CO_2 emissions by far,
Walk down to your local shop,
Buy the world a fruit lollipop.

It won't change all at once, so give it a chance,
The world wants to always be able to dance,
Do a little something every day,
Each small step goes a long, long way.

Shannon McGregor (13)
Dartford Grammar School for Girls, Dartford

Dear Anna

Dear Anna,
Do you know how lucky you are
To live in a world
That is fresh and clean?
Do you know that some people have
Nothing?

They have only extreme hunger,
They have no way out,
The people are dying,
From all sorts of diseases,
Unknown and common.

But because they don't have the right treatment,
They die,
Dear Anna, it's sad but they do,
What can we do to help?

We can donate to charities
And together buy enough
So that the people have care
And love
And schooling
And together,
We can make a difference.

Together as one.

Rachel McNally (12)
Dartford Grammar School for Girls, Dartford

Wonderful, Tropical Lands

So many creatures,
Animals galore,
They crawl, creep and prowl,
Chatter, chant and roar!

Yet the thing they fear,
They always fuss,
At the deadly, mean
Us!

For we come in
And destroy their homes,
Take it, grab it,
But they continue to roam.

We are killing our world,
We should be ashamed,
What do we want it for?
What have we got to gain?

If only we could realise
And take each others' hands,
We should really keep,
These wonderful, tropical lands.

Hazel Anne Elizabeth Millar (12)
Dartford Grammar School for Girls, Dartford

If I Could Be Prime Minister

If I could be Prime Minister,
I would stop cars polluting,
Encourage buses, trains and even cycling,
If I could be Prime Minister,
I would put up the flag of peace,
And so all killings would cease,
If I could be Prime Minister,
I would try and save the animals,
From the smallest insect to biggest mammals,
If I could be Prime Minister,
I would reduce the pay of celebs,
Giving the money to hard workers instead,
If I could be Prime Minister,
I would take care of everyone,
After all these things have happened,
My job here shall be done.

Rachel Meachin (13)
Dartford Grammar School for Girls, Dartford

Take Care Of The Rainforest

High up in the trees,
The birds are singing,
The butterflies are dancing
And the fish are swimming,
Deep in the forest the animals play,
A man with a saw is soon on his way,
More trees to be lost,
How sad this must be,
The man with his saw,
He smiles with glee,
The forest is precious,
We must take more care,
Recycle our paper,
Or the forest may be bare!

Joanne Lovett (13)
Dartford Grammar School for Girls, Dartford

Pollution

All of those factories, pumping out that smoke,
Sooner or later, we'll all start to choke!
When will we stop or is it too late?
When will we think, for goodness sake?

Now let's all be rational, not start a fight,
Turn your washers to 30° and turn out that light.

When will we think, and stop for a second,
To think about the harm we're doing
And to learn our lesson?

So let's all unite and turn down the heating,
Let's be eco-friendly,
And use all the leftovers we're not eating.

Isabel Meek (12)
Dartford Grammar School for Girls, Dartford

Green Machine

The green machine swung round,
Cutting down the sound,
Of the wild, wild east,
Where the wild bears eats.

The trees fell down,
As the green machine swung round,
Where's the wild, wild east?
No more wild bears beast.

The trees were gone,
As the green machine stopped,
No more wild, wild east,
Bye, bye, wild bear.

Lawrencia Njume (12)
Dartford Grammar School for Girls, Dartford

My Dream World

My dream world is simply impossible,
Now that buildings of dull grey stand tall,
As if they were monsters looking down upon us.
The choking fumes enclose us,
Stopping everyone and everything from experiencing the truth.
Beauty.
The forests that were once kingdoms full of magic and life
Prove nothing to be but the bones of royalty.
Destroyed, dry and dead.
Beauty.
The grand ice that grew to be mountains once
Glistened like diamonds. We melted them to liquid;
We grew the fire too powerful.
Beauty.
My scarred eyes long to heal. Only the colour and vibrancy,
Light and dark, pure and fresh, growth and birth,
Have the strength.
Beauty.
The key to nature to bud in mine eyes.
Nurturing the seed that blossoms within.
Beauty.
My dream world is simply possible, now that the velvet
Night's sky sinks to the Earth's bed,
And the sparkling stars peer through the velvet sheets.
My muscles ease but my imagination is awake,
As I sleep only to dream.
Beauty.

Tiffany Winthrop (16)
Dover Grammar School for Girls, Dover

Crying In The Emptiness

Waking up in the emptiness,
Only hearing my own voice,
Where are the trees?
Where are the creatures?
I cry.

Waking up in the emptiness,
Regretting all my crimes,
Causing pain and sorrow,
I cry.

Waking up in the emptiness,
Should have recycled, should have walked instead
Of burning fossil fuels,
I cry.

Waking up in the emptiness,
Thinking *what should I do? What can I do?*
To prevent the world from misery,
I cry.

What should I do when I grow up?
I want to help the environment and yet I don't,
Just think about it, which is important to us?
Money or our planet?
Money is important,
But that can't be right,
Money can't save Earth,
Only we can make a difference.

From now on, I won't wake up in the emptiness,
I'll do all I can,
Just to save our planet, with all our loved ones,
I'll try my best and I won't cry any more,
I'll smile making Earth feel brighter and lighter
And soon it will be like Heaven.

Katherine Hau (12)
Elizabeth Garrett Anderson Language College, Islington

Think About . . .

Why oh why is the world like this?
Let me tell you why it is.

I throw away in the bin,
You throw on the floor.

I'm recycling everything I can,
Bottles, cans and paper.
You're too lazy,
You throw it straight in the bin.

Get up and get ready to use your legs,
Cars are the world's worst enemies,
You want paper,
Trees miss out!

Everyone is the same as each other,
So leave people alone and treat them equally.

Poor polar bears are losing their homes,
But you don't care, do you?
Think about your grandchildren,
They will want to see one.

Why do you fight?
It's so unfair.

I'm thinking of the world,
We have hot summers,
Not hot winters.

I can throw a snowball,
In twenty years will we be able to?

So think about it!

Molly Mae Dean (11)
Elizabeth Garrett Anderson Language College, Islington

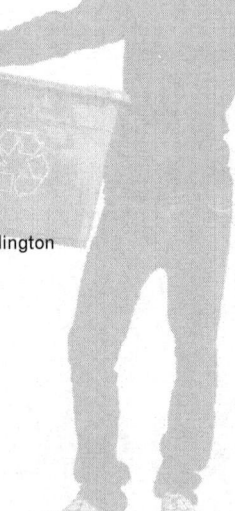

Pollution

Why is the smoke growing
And weather patterns changing?
What about the lack of rain?
Hey, what are you doing?
In the sea and Earth ruin,
Isn't polluting really insane?

The trees are bright green,
Colour of life where it has been,
So do not cut them ever down,
Or the nature will lose its crown.

The people do not care,
Surely not knowing,
Without plants we are dying,
Without the source of air.

It's really so sad,
The world is becoming so mad,
If you don't help it,
If you may not stop it,
All hope will vanish,
Our plant shall perish.

Good luck Muse,
Here is good news,
Just give it a try
And no flower will die,
The birds above will fly,
The Mother Nature will never cry,
Mankind will be saved
And no star will ever fade.

Jude Allah Maryam Seddiki (12)
Elizabeth Garrett Anderson Language College, Islington

Drip Drop Water

I'm dripping from a tap,
It's such a waste,
I could be a drink,
I could be a shower,
I could be a bath,
I could be part of a flower.

I'm dripping from a tap,
It's such a shame,
I could be in London,
I could be in Rome,
I could be in Paris,
But here I am alone.

I'm dripping from a tap,
It's such a waste,
You should twist the tap,
You should take a shower,
You could not take a bath
And not hose the flowers.

I'm dripping from a tap,
It's such a shame,
I could be a park,
I could be in the sun,
I could be a pool,
I could be such fun.

But unless you want this,
Stop wasting us drops!
Drip, drop water.

Winnie Mac (12)
Elizabeth Garrett Anderson Language College, Islington

Clumsy Weather

A breath of wind,
A flow of wind,
Growing and moaning,
Then gushing and running,
Blowing the leaves,
Fighting the trees,
Has the sun come out?
No! Here comes the rain,
Pitter, patter, drops of rain,
Splashes and splatters,
Like children do,
Then torrential rocks smash along,
Gushing down like a waterfall,
There is no sign of anything at all,
Has the sun come out?
No! Here comes the storm,
Flashing and bashing,
Crashing and smashing,
Then comes the bellowing between the trees,
As it stings the Earth like buzzing bees,
Booming and thrashing, crazy, crashing,
Then slowly, slowly . . .
Stop
Everything comes to a halt,
And nothing is anyone's fault,
Has the sun come out?

Assya Touitha (13)
Elizabeth Garrett Anderson Language College, Islington

Electricity

Switch off lights,
You'll have a great night,
If you want me to stay,
Don't waste me today,
Be happy with me or
You won't ever see me!

Niva Deb (12)
Elizabeth Garrett Anderson Language College, Islington

What A Beautiful World

What a beautiful world,
What a beautiful life,
While we live,
Nature dies.

What a beautiful year,
What beautiful months,
Species of nature are in fear
And we start our next generation clearly aware,
While nature's food's being shared,
We are greedy and don't care.

What beautiful weeks,
What beautiful days,
We pollute the air,
But the trees give us the air we need,
For vanity we do drastic things
And nature struggles for our sins.

What a beautiful hour,
What a beautiful minute,
While time runs out,
We take everything for granted.

What a beautiful second
And every second counts,
So make it worthwhile for everything and everyone.

Tamanna Sufia Ahad (11)
Elizabeth Garrett Anderson Language College, Islington

London Town

The world is meant to be green
But people don't care,
They don't care if there is a bit of dirt here or there,
We have to clean London now,
So we can have a pretty town,
Flowers, birds and bees,
Make London filled with trees.

Cherrelle Genfi (11)
Elizabeth Garrett Anderson Language College, Islington

You And Me

You and me have no differences at all,
Though why do you give me so much trouble?
First I gave you a beautiful blue sea,
But you have given pollution to me.
Next I gave nice fresh air,
But you don't even seem to care.
After, I gave you a living heart,
Then you made these poor cows fart.
You have destroyed my environment,
Now this is a big embarrassment.
So then you cut down our healthy trees,
Destroying our lands and the habitats of bees.
You mess me up with litter and oil spilling
And now rivers and lands are filling.
Reduce, reuse, recycle, are things you do right now,
But you don't even know how.
Lastly you have created global warming
And that is ungrateful and appalling,
I have now come to an end,
So *please* look after us again!

Shifa Begum (11)
Elizabeth Garrett Anderson Language College, Islington

Don't Forget Me!

Don't take the world for granted,
You're not as smart as you think,
When you die you might as well be
Planted down in your bathroom sink.
Are you using the three R's?
Are you helping the Earth?
Did you stop using cars?
What's the point in giving birth?
One day you'll all die,
But I will stand here,
Watching you throw pie
And falling with fear.

Tasnima Akther & Nadra Ahmed (12)
Elizabeth Garrett Anderson Language College, Islington

Sun Vs Rain

The sun comes out,
Without a doubt,
Drip, drip, drip down the drain,
Here comes the rain.

Sun, sun, sun,
Get your job done,
Rain, rain, go away,
Let the children come and play.

The rainbow comes out,
The children shout,
All the beautiful colours,
Go down the rainbow,
You find lots of dollars.

We need them both too,
To complete your oath,
To keep our land green,
So we can eat more beans.

Salma Yahiya (12)
Elizabeth Garrett Anderson Language College, Islington

Mrs Green

Mrs Green likes to recycle,
Her friends hate riding bicycles,
So they take the car,
And they don't even go far.

Mrs Green likes to reuse,
While others just refuse,
They make pollution everywhere,
And they don't even care.

Mrs Green likes to reduce
And buys fresh produce,
So get recycling,
To help the planet be green
And save the world from overheating.

Bobbie-Louise Burke (11)
Elizabeth Garrett Anderson Language College, Islington

The Ballad Of The Plastic Tins

Away I go into the rubbish bin,
Although I thought it was no sin,
To be a small plastic tin.

Once I was in the landfill,
It made me feel rather ill,
That I never again would be filled.

And that a few days from now,
I would be dead.

Away I go into the recycling bin,
So I could be reused again,
Oh what a life for a small plastic tin.

Once I enter the recycling centre,
I get transformed into another thing,
Like a shiny pink plastic string.

So as I say my life goes on
And I am reborn into another form.

Ruth Belai Styan (12)
Elizabeth Garrett Anderson Language College, Islington

Mother Nature And Us

I give you beehives and you take the honey to make your own money,
I take CO_2 and give you air but you just give me fire flares,
Mother Nature is me, so why can't you see, I really want to be free?
Climate change makes me feel strange,
Killing my flowers just by the hours,
I give you no trouble and you give me double!
Litter which smells so bitter should be called a sin
Or just chucked in the bin!
Rhymes and mimes won't help solve this crime,
So start helping me to be a lean, mean, green machine,
Like nature intended,
Not human recommended.

Yaneneh Isabel Ceesay Ocampo (11)
Elizabeth Garrett Anderson Language College, Islington

Wasting Something Precious

Innocent people dying of starvation
And here we are not noticing the humiliation,
They have to suffer nearly every day of the week,
We can't wait to end the week but we don't realise
We're being a freak.
Our wasting of money on food to munch,
Has created the terrible credit crunch,
If we are to change our ways,
We must follow what the right people have to say,
We can guarantee, to find herbs we won't have
To travel overseas,
If you take a shower, instead of a bath,
We can make sure you will save the needy people
Enough water to smile and laugh,
So read this poem and realise you need to make a difference,
And after that, the people who you have helped,
Won't need to be angry or tense.

Atfa Mohamed (12)
Elizabeth Garrett Anderson Language College, Islington

Humans Don't Care About Our Feelings Inside!

Thrown away in the bins, dirty and dusty,
Down, down I go blinded in black,
Then crumpled by the crushers into small pieces,
'RIP,' says my friend Zack.

Humans don't care about our feelings inside,
Unimportant - worthless,
Every day we're used and every day we're thrown,
But that's life I guess.

Sometimes I wish life could be better,
Easy, happy and nice,
People would reuse me,
Instead of leaving me to rot with mice.

Masuma Khanom (12)
Elizabeth Garrett Anderson Language College, Islington

Four Seasons

There's four seasons for a reason, not just for fun,
So make sure you know them my little hun!

The four seasons are winter, autumn, spring and summer,
It's good to know them and don't get dumber.

Summer may be very hot,
Winter may be very cold.

In springtime all the flowers bloom,
In autumn time, the leaves start to fall.

But wouldn't it be weird if summer was cold
And winter was hot?

Vicky Lam (12)
Elizabeth Garrett Anderson Language College, Islington

Gone

I'm dying, help save me,
It's all rotting away,
I need light,
My leaves are falling
And you just keep on sailing,
They can't stay up,
The trees go boo to all those people that don't have a clue,
Don't just leave us here,
We'll pass out, come quick,
There's still some time,
Just come help!

Maliha Chowdhury (11)
Elizabeth Garrett Anderson Language College, Islington

Save The Earth

I want this Earth to be green,
But some people are stingy and mean,
I really want to reach my goal,
If you help me, an Eco-kid is your new role!
I'll encourage people not to use cars,
The result will be as big as from here to Mars,
I'll discourage people to litter,
By telling them that they could kill an animal - that is bitter,
I want this Earth to be green,
But some people are stingy and mean,
Save the Earth!

Probha Zannat Chowdhury (11)
Elizabeth Garrett Anderson Language College, Islington

I Am

I am the one who gives you water,
I am the one who gives you air,
I am the one who gives you land,
I am the one who gives you pears,
I am the one who gives you trees,
I am the one who gives you peace,
I am the one who gives you sunlight,
You just give me carbon dioxide,
I am the world, you're the people
That live in me, so please take care of me.

Jamirys Dos Santos Craveiro (12)
Elizabeth Garrett Anderson Language College, Islington

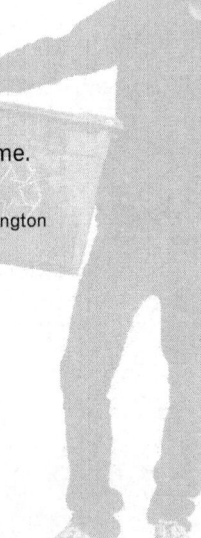

Recycle . . . How Do You Recycle?

Recycling, how hard could it be?
It's just like making a cup of tea,
Metals, plastics and other things too,
Collect them all and use them for you,
Help me save the world, I say,
It's not like a game I have to play,
I love saving, it's so fun,
I think I have saved a ton,
Now I know how to stay green,
I feel so good and part of a team.

Gabriele Watts (12)
Elizabeth Garrett Anderson Language College, Islington

The Green Tree

Nature, nature,
Why can't we all be green?
Why do people have to be so mean?
I doubt nature is here to stay,
It will probably be gone by May!
Paper, plastic, card and cans,
We really should do a national ban,
Turn off the lights, turn off the taps
And put London on the maps.

Maya Kesang Bajracharya (12)
Elizabeth Garrett Anderson Language College, Islington

The Earth

I'm the one, the one and only,
I'm the one, you keep me lonely,
I pray and pray every day
For the people to care for me,
Treat me like a star,
Oh the prayers that I pray and for what?
I'm the Earth, that's me,
I'm the one that keeps you alive,
You can't live without me.

Sanaa El-Waouzi (11)
Elizabeth Garrett Anderson Language College, Islington

I Remember . . .

I remember the days when only trees I could see,
I remember when everything was green,
Before pollution and before war,
It was always a pretty picture, always a pretty sight,
I loved seeing the birds fly so high,
I loved seeing the animals be free and wild,
I remember those days those beautiful days.

Sarah Elawad (12)
Islamia Girls' School, London

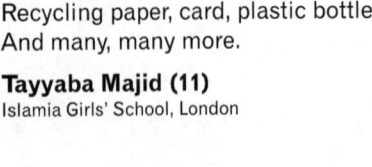

Recycling

Recycling is helpful,
Environmentally friendly,
Helping each other,
Making it a better place,
Recycling paper, card, plastic bottles
And many, many more.

Tayyaba Majid (11)
Islamia Girls' School, London

I Don't Understand

I don't understand why,
People lie?
People die?

I don't understand why,
The children of Africa must starve?
The colours of our skin are split in to half?

I don't understand why,
A child of five must walk miles to find water?
We must slaughter?

I don't understand why,
Some people don't give up their seat?
Some can't or won't eat?

I don't understand why,
Some say hurtful things?
And why others do the killings?

I'm not sure if I will ever understand why we do these things.

All I wish is that one person would find out why and
Find out how we can fix it.

Sarah Dowding (15)
Marjorie McClure School, Chislehurst

Save Water And Stop The Floods

You have got to keep watching,
Stop using your car - save petrol,
Take a walk in the woods,
We might see some birds,
We might see some foxes,
We might see some rabbits,
But if you keep on using your cars,
You won't see them anymore.

Hannah Manston (13)
Marjorie McClure School, Chislehurst

Wonderful World

W hat will make the world an even better place than it is already?
O ne day we all get up and the environment is clean and tidy,
N o wars,
D ifferent is OK,
E verybody is treated equally, no matter what creed, colour, disability,
R ecent money troubles were pretend,
F rogs and other animals are not extinct,
U nicorns are real,
L ovely weather all year round in England,

W hales and dolphins are not dying,
O ne day the world is at peace,
R oaring lions carry on living,
L ovely, happy children are heard all the time,
D ear tiny babies are not stillborn.

Elizabeth Howard (17)
Marjorie McClure School, Chislehurst

Save Animals

Stop killing animals!
I wish it were me,
Angry,
Remember this,
Listen,
Understand,
Look,
Be clever,
Uncomfortable,
Safe,
Lonely,
Peer pressure.

Jason Campbell (14)
Marjorie McClure School, Chislehurst

Green World

Green, green, beautiful world, just like the world should be.

Love Mother Nature,
Like Mother Nature,
Care for Mother Nature.

So what right do we have to kill
Mother
Nature?

Jordan Findlay (16)
Marjorie McClure School, Chislehurst

Keep Animals Alive

Keep animals healthy, take them to the vet when they are poorly,

Fed your pet every day and give them some water.

Make sure your animals get some exercise.

And give your animal some love.

Stephanie Brown-Redford (12)
Marjorie McClure School, Chislehurst

Racism

Black, white, Asian, African,
Why can't people understand?
Beneath the skin lies the same,
Red blood, lungs, liver, beating heart.
Christian, Muslim, Jewish, Sikh,
Beliefs all differ,
Beneath the skin lies the same,
Red blood, lungs, liver, beating heart.
See the difference, have the difference,
Names, thump, kick, kill,
See the same, understand the difference.
Peace, love, harmony, tranquillity.

Samuel Piddock (11)
Rainham Mark Grammar School, Rainham

What You Gonna Do?

CO_2
Not good for you,
It can harm all the nature on Earth,
It can also harm you,
So what you gonna do?
Co_2 is not good for you.

Recycle and reuse,
You've got to choose,
A way to save the Earth,
It is a good thing for you,
So what you gonna do?
Recycle and reuse.

The rainforest needs saving,
We need to start behaving
And use less paper now,
This is sure to help you,
So what you gonna do?
The rainforest needs saving.

There's too much litter,
It's making life bitter
And harms the environment,
It is not good for you,
So what you gonna do?
There's too much litter.

Erin Jackson (12)
Rainham Mark Grammar School, Rainham

Why Not?

Why not recycle?
Why not save the world?
If you're about to get in the car, why not just cycle?
It stops pollution,
It saves us,
So I say never catch the bus!
Why not walk?

Paige Roger (11)
Rainham Mark Grammar School, Rainham

The Problems With The World

Some might be tall,
Some might be small,
But they have never hurt us,
So why do we cut them down?

The world is our home,
We are all family,
So what is the point of wars?

Recycle, recycle, recycle!
That's all I ever hear,
I do my best
And so should you!

Some people are hungry,
Some people are lonely
And some have no money,
But they are all homeless,
So now we must help them.

Jordan Vaughan (11)
Rainham Mark Grammar School, Rainham

A World, A Place, A Problem, Poverty!

A world where those are homeless,
A world where people die every three seconds,
A world where people have no medication,
A world where they have no money for food or drink,
A place which people forget,
A place where people live on the streets,
A place where people suffer from disease,
A place where those struggle to live,
A place where families are close together,
A problem all over the world,
A problem not very pleasant,
A problem that can be prevented,
A problem, that we can help . . . stop!

Rhiannon Truscott (11)
Rainham Mark Grammar School, Rainham

Green Glorious Ground

Is litter bad?
Why are animals extinct?
Can we stop it now?

Why do we do it?
Do we need animal skins?
Can we stop it now?

Do your bit to help,
Tell talking people as well,
So can we stop it?

Working together,
Helps the world unite right,
So can we stop it?

Working together,
Work as one, work together,
So we can stop it!

Lauren Davis (11)
Rainham Mark Grammar School, Rainham

What Happened To The World?

What happened to the world all those years ago?
Where did we go wrong?
Where are the polar bears, the blue sky, the snow?
What happened to the world that we used to know?
What happened to those crisp winter mornings?
Did we never see the warnings?

What happened to the world all those years ago?
Where did we go wrong?
Where are the rivers that ran clear?
Where are the trees, the chimpanzees, the wild birds
Or the orang-utans?
Where did the wild birds, the bees or whales go?
How can we take a mouse and rearrange is features?
What are we doing to all these poor creatures?

Rosalind Walker (11)
Rainham Mark Grammar School, Rainham

Problems Of The World!

There is a start and end to this word pollution,
It means a lot of things,
Though really we need a solution.

Such beautiful whales,
Being killed every day,
There is no one to blame,
But ourselves, we must pay.

One major thing is,
Litter being dropped,
There is no excuse,
It can be stopped.

People left stranded,
Around the world they're homeless,
No shelter for them,
Yet still we are not blameless.

Lucy Buck (11)
Rainham Mark Grammar School, Rainham

Let's Go Sailing

It was on that day,
When the sky was blue,
Flowers were out
And the young larks flew.

That we set sail,
For my first time,
Out into the sea,
It was calm and still,
But fate was yet to turn.

But what greeted us was not what I thought,
A sea of litter,
Swaying in the waves,
My eyes were opened,
I didn't want to litter anymore
And wanted no one else to.

Isaac John Cawte (11)
Rainham Mark Grammar School, Rainham

Save Our Planet

What is happening to our planet?
What are you doing about it?
Do you drive,
Or save lives?

What is happening to our planet?
What are you doing about it?
Will you do something about it
Or will you forget about it?

What is happening to our planet?
What are you doing about it?
Be a hero,
Or be a zero.
Simple things can make a change,
All you have to do is listen.
Save our planet.

Matthew Leach (11)
Rainham Mark Grammar School, Rainham

The Environment

E nergy is widely overused,
N ations come together to bring good news,
V ans and cars are polluting our air,
I try to show we all must care,
R un, I ride, it's so much better,
O n this planet was a wonderful place,
N ow it's just a big disgrace,
M an, come on, we just don't care,
E ven though our trees are dying,
N ow our icebergs and Arctic are truly frying,
T hat means that polar bears are still crying.

We know all these things
Are going on but we still don't
Stop, look, act and change.

Harvey Sanderson (11)
Rainham Mark Grammar School, Rainham

Our Input

There's crystal snow on mountains,
Then icebergs slowly fading,
Pure fresh air we breathe,
Pollution which we place into it.

New creatures being discovered,
Others we place under threat,
Peace and happiness in one place,
War and death somewhere else.

Seeds growing harmlessly in the ground,
Trees slowly being cut down,
People warm in a house where they live,
But then still many left in the cold.

What has become of our world?

Abigail Grootveld (11)
Rainham Mark Grammar School, Rainham

The Rainforest

I trek through the rainforest,
No one in sight, I trek throughout the day
And all through the night.

I see a parrot here and
Another one there but
Soon it will be gone
With no one to care.

The acid rain destroys it all,
Animal extinction's the next call.

I'm sad to say,
It's time to go,
To leave this beautiful world
We will never know.

Chelsea Benham (12)
Rainham Mark Grammar School, Rainham

Laziness

When you look out the window,
What do you see?
A happy world,
Where everyone is free?
Or do you see pollution,
Knocking at the door?
But who is gonna answer, help?
Not you that's for sure,
We all knew it was coming,
All we did was sit and cry,
Help us! Save us! Help us!
You might as well just hop it,
If you don't like what is going on,
Then why don't you try to stop it?

Harry Charles Alexander Palmer (11)
Rainham Mark Grammar School, Rainham

Our World

Children are starving all around,
Nothing on their faces but a frown.

Animals run and look in panic,
As one of their trees get struck down.

Our world should be a happy place,
Where none are frowning,
All are smiling,
The way our world should be.

Greed is a bad thing, we take from people
Who have nothing, if paper is needed, recycling can be done.

So let's all work together and make the world a brighter place
For all the starving children and the human race.

Nadine Orhiere (11)
Rainham Mark Grammar School, Rainham

Global Warming!

G ross affects
L ush meadows are ruined,
O bservations aren't lovely anymore,
B rilliant ice worlds are ruined,
A wful rivers,
L andscapes are horrible.

W e ruin trees and we're ruining us,
A mazing animals lose their habitats,
R oyals discuss these awful issues,
M uddy fields,
 I magine what could happen,
N ow global warming is down to you,
G ross lakes.

Luke Fitzmaurice (11)
Rainham Mark Grammar School, Rainham

I Can't Remember

I can't remember a cold winter with heavy snow,
I can't remember when it snowed in winter,
The last time it snowed was April!
I can't remember when we last had a hot summer,
Now it's all rainy and wet,
I can't remember some of the animals as some have gone extinct,
I can't remember a nice flowing lake, or sea,
Now they are polluted and full of litter,
I can't remember when the world made friends,
Now there are always wars and fights,
I can't remember a clear ground,
Now it's all buried under litter and plants.

Isn't it sad I can't remember?

Emily Smyth (11)
Rainham Mark Grammar School, Rainham

Litterbug

Are you the litterbug
Crawling round our streets?
Looking for something dead and unwanted to eat?

Are you the litterbug,
Who needs to know what a bin is used for?
As all you do is hide behind a door.

Are you the litterbug,
That tries to harm the environment?
Who never tries something new to help their country?

Don't turn into the litterbug,
Do you want to be known as the litterbug?
Think about it . . .

Darcy Baldwin (11)
Rainham Mark Grammar School, Rainham

Poverty

Poverty is everywhere,
Hanging around in the air,
Huts and shacks and things like that
And sometimes nowhere at all,
Their crying faces, their weary eyes,
It's mean for us to tell a lie,
They live in dust, from dawn till dusk
And never one complaint.
No Christmas presents or turkey,
They're hungry and they're thirsty,
But no one here could give a care,
To think . . .
Poverty is everywhere.

Bethany Wood (11)
Rainham Mark Grammar School, Rainham

Planet Poem

Our ozone layer is so thin,
So put your rubbish in the recycle bin,
Acid rain, you're a pain,
When you hit my windowpane,
Hurricanes come and go,
Wrecking things as they blow,
Forests are being cut,
Which gives me a bad feeling in my gut,
Seeing litter makes me feel bitter,
Living on the street,
Your life must be so bleak,
Don't call names,
It's not a war!

Scott York (11)
Rainham Mark Grammar School, Rainham

War World

The world is full of war,
There is so much slaughtering,
So much blood and gore,
Soon we have to act,
Or everyone will die
And that's a fact,
The world is slowly dying,
No one is doing anything,
No one is even trying,
If we kill off this world now,
Nothing to eat,
Nothing to chew,
The world is full of war.

Emmanuel Akinso (11)
Rainham Mark Grammar School, Rainham

Rain And Shine

I am the carer, you are the killer,
I am the maker, you are the destroyer,
I am the freshness, you are the polluter,
I gave you richness, you wasted the present.

Some people live in a beautiful world,
Some people live in a dull and black world,
Some people are full of delight,
Some people are full of anger.

People can sometimes be full of fun,
People can sometimes be full of love,
But people are always full of heart and
Happiness whatever happens.

Andrew France (11)
Rainham Mark Grammar School, Rainham

What Have We Done?

In the beginning God created the world,
He created it with love and care,
In the beginning He gave us clean water,
In the beginning God gave us fresh air.

God gave us mountains, valleys and rivers,
God gave us deserts, green land and lakes,
God then made humans
And we made our mistake.

We created pollution and litter,
We destroyed rainforests and made animals extinct,
We made climate change, poverty and war,
If only we had stopped to think.

Samuel Atkins (11)
Rainham Mark Grammar School, Rainham

Why? Why? Why?

Where are all the animals?
Where are all the trees?
Why is it so hot in here?
Why does my mum cough so hard?

Why are people living on the streets?
Why are there bombs?
Why do people be mean to black people?
Why do people pollute our air?

Why? Why? Why?
For all of these things I do not know,
But if we all work together,
We can make a difference.

Samuel Peters (11)
Rainham Mark Grammar School, Rainham

The Poor And Homeless

There was a man called Jeffery,
He had nowhere to stay,
But all the children of the Earth,
Just laughed at his pain,
But what if they were homeless?
Would they still be laughing?

There was a man called Jeremy,
He was ever so poor,
But all the children of the Earth,
Just couldn't care anymore,
But what if they were poor?
Would they still be laughing?

Steven Denny (11)
Rainham Mark Grammar School, Rainham

The Power Of Green

CO_2, carbon footprint, all about the world,
All of these things make the greenhouse gases swirl,
Not wasting water, turning the lights off,
Knowing that saves energy, you don't have to be a boff,
To know that we have saved our Earth
And started saving it from birth
And in all we can confide,
We saved the planet.

Green is for recycling every day and night,
The energy it does save may give you a fright,
So know of the power of green,
Use it to keep our world clean . . .

Alex Heard (11)
Rainham Mark Grammar School, Rainham

They're So Hungry!

Folk are hungry,
They must be so lonely,
They've got no money,
Do we have too much?
So, come on, let's help them,
Those adults and children,
Those ravenous bellies,
Not eating enough,
The world is crying and
People are dying,
While many do nothing,
Put poverty to an end.

Daniel Barnes (11)
Rainham Mark Grammar School, Rainham

The World's Dying

The world's dying but do we know,
One day the world's going to go,
Soon, soon we have to act,
We have to think fast and that's a fact,
Think of the people that are new to this world,
All the baby boys and all the baby girls,
They have to live a life like all the others,
What about your sisters and brothers?
So come on, do your bit,
Or the world is going to end up like a tip,
The world's dying!

James Busby (11)
Rainham Mark Grammar School, Rainham

War And Peace

Wars are destroying my planet,
Everything I gave to you,
You are destroying with your selfless hate,
Where has any peace gone that you might have had?
War! A word meaning destruction and loss,
Peace! Calm, loving . . .
And for the few people who care,
If we all stick together,
We can stop destruction and hate,
We can make the world a better place,
We can be free.

Kerry Boughton (11)
Rainham Mark Grammar School, Rainham

Global Warming - Haiku

Animals have died,
Ice caps melting one by one,
A carcass floats by.

Eve Michell (11)
Rainham Mark Grammar School, Rainham

73

Homeless

Homeless and alone, he has no home,
Searching for shelter, his life is a helter-skelter,
Spiralling down he wants to drown,
Begging for money to buy some honey,
He starts to cry, he wants his mummy,
Then he thinks of something funny,
He thinks of brighter days,
But they seem such a haze,
As he closes his eyes lying on cold rubble,
He gives thanks, at least he is not in trouble.

Harleigh Yvonne Stephens (11)
Rainham Mark Grammar School, Rainham

About Our World

In our world today,
We need an answer to the pollution,
And recycling of our litter,
May be part of the solution.

With all the poverty, hate and war,
Sometimes it's hard to work out what we are fighting for.

Maybe if everyone would work together,
The climate change, poverty and homelessness
Would get much better.

William Brittain (11)
Rainham Mark Grammar School, Rainham

Governments Don't Help!

As the rivers keep on rising,
At a rate that is surprising,
The ice caps will shrink,
Whilst governments think,
More problems on the horizon.

Scott Shillabeer (11)
Rainham Mark Grammar School, Rainham

The World Around Us

R ows were sparked when white and black were pushed apart,
A multitude of black people protested, rioted and supported
  Nelson Mandela,
C rowds of people protested to stop it,
I nstead of peace and fairness, black people were treated
  Differently to whites,
S egregation, separation and discrimination were unnecessary,
M ost ethnic groups and minorities have learnt to live with
  Each other.

Emmanuel Ayomoto (12)
Rainham Mark Grammar School, Rainham

Recycle

R euse, recycle, recreate,
E nvironmental ways of helping the world,
C ool way of recycling,
Y ou can do anything you set your mind to,
C an you make a difference?
L earn about the world,
I nvent new ways of recycling,
N ow can you,
G et together to help save the world?

Darren Matthews (11)
Rainham Mark Grammar School, Rainham

You Give Me

You give me rainforests and animals to live,
I give extinction and crumbling cliffs!

You give me food, water and fun,
I give you poverty, racism and that's only some.

You give me populations, difference and love,
I give you war, bombs . . . and that's enough!

Pierce Coveney (11)
Rainham Mark Grammar School, Rainham

Help!

R ecycle if recyclable,
E verybody could help,
C limate change is here,
Y ou can make a difference,
C hange the way you think,
L ook after the world,
I ce caps are melting,
N ow is your time to act,
G o and help the world!

David Winchester (11)
Rainham Mark Grammar School, Rainham

Every Time In War

Every time there is speeches,
Every time there is tanks,
Every time there is battles,
Every time bombers bomb,
Every time ships set sail,
Every time bullets fly,
Every time there is refugees,
Every time people die,
Every time there is hope.

Mark Coomber (12)
Rainham Mark Grammar School, Rainham

The Wasteful Planet

The trees are being cut down,
Litter is found more and more,
All of this wants to make me frown,
I wish we could open a new door.

If anybody can hear me,
We need to put a stop to it,
So let's save the trees,
Let's all change and make this a big hit.

Jasmin Kaur (11)
Rainham Mark Grammar School, Rainham

Where Are All The Animals Going?

Where are all the animals going?
I can't find them anywhere
There aren't any monkeys,
Swinging from tree to tree,
There are no giant whales,
Making huge splashes,
Where are all the animals going?
I can't find them anywhere.

Ryan Hales (11)
Rainham Mark Grammar School, Rainham

Help!

War blood is red,
Pollution is grey,
Being homeless and poor,
Causes dismay,
So think about these things
And maybe we could,
Help the homeless and poor,
I think we should.

Jonathan Murphy (11)
Rainham Mark Grammar School, Rainham

What About

Where are we?
Lost and alone,
Nowhere to go.

Where are we?
Lost and alone,
Destroying ourselves.

Where are we?
Lost and alone,
With sadness in the world.

Where are we?
Lost and alone,
Nothing healthy, nowhere to go.

Where are we?
Lost and alone,
Surrounded in sadness.

Where are we?
Lost and alone,
What to do?

Where are we?
Lost and alone,
I know I am not on Earth.

What can we do?
Save the world,
Save the world.

Tannita Stokes (11)
St George's RC School, Maida Vale

Animals = Extinction

Hunters kill day and night although they know it's not right,
Animals are going very fast, now you don't see many birds go past,
Hunters kill loads a day, even though 'We don't like it,'
That's what we say,
We could moan and groan but still they skin them to the bone.

Adam Cotter (11)
St George's RC School, Maida Vale

Life By Living

You have a world,
So beautiful and clean,
Humanity as one,
Working together in a team.

You have a world,
Plants grow and we live freely,
Farmers live in houses, milking cows,
It might sound boring, but it's nice really.

You have a world,
The sun glows bright,
The moon lights the evening,
It all happens by day and night.

You have a world,
It breathes and it lives as well,
It exists you know
And it's rather swell.

You have a world,
But you pollute it slowly enough,
Soon it will be gone,
Why must you be so rough?

You had a world,
But now it is gone,
Stop this pollution,
It's extremely wrong.

Daniel Ahern (11)
St George's RC School, Maida Vale

What A World?

Butchered rainforests,
What have we done?
Pure toxic air,
What have we done?
$CH_2 SO_4$,
What have we done?
A burning hot winter,
What have we done?
Ultimatum for polar bears' lives,
What have we done?
Shared among the ground corpses,
What have we done?
Black's wrong: White's right?
What have we done?
10 years on cardboard,
What have we done?
Bitter sweet lollies,
What have we done?
New sun's cruel kindness,
What have we done?
A calm sea,
What have we done?
Now or never: never now,
Why don't we do?
Global warming - sad and true,
What can we do?

Mél M Azombo (14)
St George's RC School, Maida Vale

In Return

I give you a place to live,
You give me trash.

I give you a good ambience,
You give me destruction.

The ground is infected,
The air is polluted.

I give you forests,
You give me flames,
I give you air,
You give me poisonous gas.

The forests are burning,
The icicles are parting.

I give you ground,
You give me explosions,
I give you a sky,
You give me madness.

The ice is melting,
I try to react,
But you do not stop,
And I'm being destroyed.

Lino Crelier (11)
St George's RC School, Maida Vale

Stop Killing All The Animals

Stop killing all the animals,
Stop polluting our fresh air,
Stop starving all the sheep and cutting off the their hair,
Every now and then, we keep cloning our fresh hens,
Stop cutting down our trees, we need a nice breeze,
Even though we need paper, it's something we could use later,
But I'll tell you something mate, you can't kill,
What you could never create!

Rianna Thompson-Quartey (11)
St George's RC School, Maida Vale

What Have We Done?

(Inspired by 'Earth Song' by Michael Jackson)

What have we done to the world?
Look what we've done.
What about all the peace we had before?
Now it's all gone to war.

Do you ever stop to notice,
What you've done?
Do you ever stop to notice,
All the children and babies dead?

What about the seas?
Pollution, pollution, dark.

What about animals dying in our faces?

Children dying,
Do you hear them cry?

What about the death again?
Do you give a damn?

Deborah Belalo (11)
St George's RC School, Maida Vale

Crime!

Knife and guns are used nearly every day,
By youths and teenagers everywhere,
Killed and stabbed on the streets,
Next day, all over the newspaper and TV.

Parents and families all in tears,
Politicians and governments try to put a stop to it,
But it keeps happening to anyone,
On streets,
In bars,
In countryside,
In school.

A crime is caused everywhere.

Ganzaya Munkhbayar (11)
St George's RC School, Maida Vale

It All Comes From Your Hands

Knife, I feel penetrate my heart,
Knife, you feel penetrate your heart,
Knife, I destroy,
Knife, you destroy
And it all comes from your hands.
Smoke, I breathe,
Smoke, you breathe,
Smoke, I stop,
Smoke, you stop,
And it all comes from your hands.
Home, I don't have,
Home, you don't have,
Home, I have,
Home you have,
And it all comes from your hands,
World that we have hurt,
World that we can save,
And it all comes from our hands.

Enery Asensio Mejia (11)
St George's RC School, Maida Vale

Pollution

As well as a stop to violence,
Put a stop to pollution,
The fumes are causing the ice caps to melt,
Whilst the flames are melting the planet,
The water is rising onto the land
And turning land into water,
The sun is causing even more pollution,
Whilst all the cars are letting out fumes
And those fumes are what causes pollution
And pollution causes global warming,
Animals are being driven out of their natural places
In the Antarctic, into hot places where they die,
Because all humans are relaxing,
They do not care about anything but themselves.

Jack Long (12)
St George's RC School, Maida Vale

83

I See

I see the police,
I see him,
He ruins the community,
An eyesore to the environment,
As the public go on with their Christmas shopping,
He is told to move on,
I see him step out of the doorway,
Hungry and cold, what can I do?
I see him look at me and I quickly turn away,
I carry on walking,
I hear a groan and look back,
Just in time to see him fall to the ground,
I run back and see his face turn blue,
I am too late!
Why didn't I help him?
I fall to the ground and the tears come,
Why didn't I help him?
Selfish I know.

Imogen Donaldson-Brown (13)
St George's RC School, Maida Vale

Give, Take

I give you money,
You buy a knife,
I give you clothes,
You give me cuts,
I give you shelter,
You give me broken hearts,
I give you love,
You give me fear,
I give you peace,
You give me anger,
I give you life,
You give me death.

Rhys Samuel Lowe (12)
St George's RC School, Maida Vale

I Give

I give you health,
You give me sickness,
I give you wealth,
You give me poverty.

I give you clean water,
You give me dirty rivers,
I give you fresh air,
You give me polluted odours.

I give you a rose,
You give me an empty cola can,
I give you a polar bear,
You give me a real fur coat.

I give you respect,
You give me disgust,
I give you one reason to stop this huge mess,
And you go 'Blah, blah, blah!'

Faten Abdel-Rahman (12)
St George's RC School, Maida Vale

Our World

The world is never silent,
with the wars and violence
and racism around.
People living in poverty
and some even homeless.
Animals becoming extinct,
with hunting and pollution.
Rainforests are dying,
the climate always changing.
Go green and recycle,
don't litter all about!

Nathania Dacosta-Hyman (11)
St George's RC School, Maida Vale

Knife And Gun Crime

Knives
And guns,
Are very
Bad. They
Cause
Problems and
Make you
Sad. People
Die and
People suffer,
The criminals
Get rougher
And rougher.
The criminals go to prison but
The streets
Don't get
Rinsed clean.

Ronniel James Adap (12)
St George's RC School, Maida Vale

Polluted

Fresh clean air,
But smoky polluted oxygen,
Trees and beautiful plants,
But dead leaves and fallen trunks.

Happy and very healthy people,
But ill and asthmatic,
Crystal clear water,
But poisonous rivers.

Warm and lively Earth,
But dangerous and polluted.

Liezelle Anne Pagala (11)
St George's RC School, Maida Vale

Litter Thrown Away

Why can't we just throw rubbish away,
Rather than pay a fine and walk away?
Help the poor and pay them much more,
Give them food to enjoy.

Don't just throw litter on the floor,
So save the Earth and be healthy,
So your future won't be lonely.

Amir Ibrahim (12)
St George's RC School, Maida Vale

Gun + Knife Crime

Gun + knives don't get along,
What's with these postcodes?
Where do I belong?
Bring the armies,
Get the police,
All we want is genuine
Peace!

Jose Rego (12)
St George's RC School, Maida Vale

Pollution

The environment is very important,
You should take great care of it,
If you pollute, you are harming yourself,
So don't pollute, because it's dangerous,
You should care about global warming,
Because as you read this poem,
There are icebergs crashing and tumbling,
So don't pollute - the choice is yours.

Harry Noble (13)
St Lawrence College, Ramsgate

Our Environment

The air we breathe in,
Is contaminated,
The waters in rivers is polluted
And global warming,
Is slowly increasing.

The environment we had years ago,
Has changed,
Our vegetation has highly reduced,
And some of our seas are drying up.

In some countries,
The environment is not taken care of,
Litter is dropped all over the floor,
The fumes of cars are polluting the air
And most of the soil is being eroded.

People are dying,
Because of our horrible environment,
What is the solution to pollution?
What is the solution to erosion?
And what is the solution to contamination?

What should we do,
To help the environment?
We should not drop litter on the floor,
We should try not to pollute the air,
And we should not waste water.

The world could be destroyed,
Because of the environment,
And if we don't take action now,
It will soon be the end.

Oluwademilade Amos-Oluwole (11)
St Lawrence College, Ramsgate

Would We Know?

If rivers became bathed in oil,
And the crippled sun started to foil,
Would we know that this is real?
How would you feel?

If thunderstorms got worse and worse
And our floodgates began to burst,
Would we know this is real?
How would you feel?

If buildings began to creak
And sewers suddenly began to leak,
Would we know this is real?
How would you feel?

If cars drove more and more,
Their harmful gases would pour and pour,
Would we know this is real?
How would you feel?

Perhaps our world will get hijacked,
If Man is to survive, we need to act,
Would we know our world is about to go!

Matt Rosier (12)
St Lawrence College, Ramsgate

World!

The trees and grass, fresh and green,
The flowers and rivers flowing and moving gently,
Flamingos and orchids moving very wonderfully,
Butterflies and dragonflies gorgeously whizzing
Around with amazing colours,
Fishes are the kings and queens of beaches
And the multicolours of the seas,
Lions and tigers control the kingdom,
They are sweet stunners,
Oh my, oh my, what pretty things,
The world is truly wonderful.

Lorna Kae Drury (12)
St Lawrence College, Ramsgate

Environment

A dolphin saw a whaling ship and shook its pointy head,
You'd think they would put their million into a tuna boat instead,
It's typical of humans, they're so greedy and crude,
Not very smart to look at what is or isn't food.

I've seen them hunting shark and throwing away all but fins,
It's such a waste and they should be punished for that sin,
God gave them salmon, mackerel and sardines to be canned,
Why do they want a whale? I don't understand.

The shoreline is ruined and no one really cares,
To keep a food chain going they must have breeders there,
But they never stop and don't look at the cost,
They only care when the species is lost.

Two hundred animals extinct, how many more will go?
Don't bother asking they don't seem to know,
Money is the only thing people think about these days,
They won't embrace a new idea unless they're sure it pays.

Sandip Rai (12)
St Lawrence College, Ramsgate

Saving Nature

Just think of the rolling plains,
Greatly beautiful and full of rain,
To the humans, this place hasn't gone in vain,
They've hunted the great lion for his mane,
Even though they're already tame,
Is their brain so lame,
That they think this is a game?
Now think of the jungle,
How the trees are in a tangle
And the way monkeys dangle,
We should protect these things
And save the animal beings,
Like an owl protects her young with her wings,
So come on,
Let's save 'em, run!

Santiago Piedras (13)
St Lawrence College, Ramsgate

90

Environmental Poem

Have you ever wondered what life is about?
You could search the world and never figure it out.

Just think how much water we throw away
And pour down the sink each day.

We should not brush our teeth under running water,
Which is what my mother tells her daughter!

The water that goes down the drain could help
People from other countries that do not have rain.

Rubbish like nets and oil that go in the sea,
Kills fish and birds and upsets me.

So we should all take care with things that we do
And the environment would be better for me and *you!*

Olivia Keel (12)
St Lawrence College, Ramsgate

The Environment

The Amazon is getting cut down,
If we don't stop now our children will suffer,
We don't want them to suffer,
So start thinking and stop chopping.

The animals are losing their homes,
Because people aren't thinking,
Like the bugs, monkeys and jaguars,
People like to see the animals and go to the Amazon.

If people don't think about it,
Then they will lose oxygen,
Like we all will because
The trees are lungs of our planet,
Start thinking, stop chopping.

Jamie Welborn (12)
St Lawrence College, Ramsgate

Stop It Now

Dropping litter,
Stop it now.

Dumping waste,
Stop it now.

Wasting paper,
Stop it now.

Wasting food,
Stop it now.

Stop it now, help Mother Earth and nature,
Don't be evil,
Stop it . . . *now!*

Uche Eboka (12)
St Lawrence College, Ramsgate

Environmental Poem

Pollution, pollution, what's the solution?
Don't litter, it makes us so bitter,
Pick up your tin and put it in the bin.

Pollution, pollution, what's the solution?
Don't chop down the trees,
Or I'll push you onto your knees.

Pollution, pollution, what's the solution?
Don't waste paper or I'll see you later!

Pollution, pollution, whatever is the solution?
Don't let our world get trashed,
Or you'll get bashed.

Emily Mills (13)
St Lawrence College, Ramsgate

Don't Spoil Our Environment

Don't pollute,
Don't ruin the environment,
Keep all clean
And don't litter
And especially don't dump in lakes.

Don't cut down trees without sustaining,
Keep your litter to yourself and recycle too,
If you don't do this, there will be consequences too.

Save the Earth by cleaning up your mess,
Sustain, recycle and don't pollute,
Look after your environment and surroundings.

Robert Mills (13)
St Lawrence College, Ramsgate

The Save The Earth Poem

Smoke, smoke everywhere, you will kill the Earth,
Gas, gas everywhere, you will kill the Earth,
Rubbish, rubbish everywhere, you will kill the Earth,
Recycle, recycle everywhere, you will
Save the Earth!

James Johnston (12)
St Lawrence College, Ramsgate

Litter Poem

If you love to litter, the world will become so bitter.
For you the world will be a disaster,
you will be the litter master.
It would be hard to believe, everyone would like you to leave.
So why don't you try something new?
What have you got to lose?
Put your litter in the bin,
it's you that has to choose.

Teresa O'Reilly (11)
St Michael's RC School, Bermondsey

The LEDC World

Poverty, a word, a cause,
A journey with no applause, no happiness within.

Poverty,
So many speak, few souls listen,
Pound in the tin, conscience in pocket, no one around.

Poverty,
They take my voice, ignore my words,
But people live in much worse conditions than you and I.

Poverty,
Level the scales, balance the need,
Enough for everyone, no time for greed.

Poverty,
The latest dance, do you hear the rhythm?
Do you know the rhyme or the crime?

Poverty,
Words that explode, none of them are mine,
Poverty to history, injustice will not confine.

Poverty,
'Make poverty history' sounds so divine,
If it soothes your conscience, fine.

Poverty,
I should be grateful shouldn't I?
Not raise questions, but learn to die.

Poverty,
Sweet charity, blind indifference,
Do you know me? Can you see me?
Will you hear me or will you ever help me?

Poverty the worst element of life,
Shall it ever leave the poor souls who bear the unwanted pain,
Of getting up in the morning and seeing no good?

Make poverty history!

Shaji Chiarelli (11)
St Michael's RC School, Bermondsey

Rainforest Rage

Bang! One tree down,
Bang! Bang! Two trees down,
Bang! Bang! Bang . . . no more trees,
No more animals,
You destroy our world.

Why?
Don't you care?
You don't care if you, me,
Friends, family or animals die!
Cutting down trees.

It's not just me,
I try my best,
You gotta see?
I don't enjoy my job,
To hire people.

Why do you hire people,
To cut down trees?
If you don't enjoy it,
Find another job!
Animals are dying,
Habitats are being destroyed,
You have to stop.

I'll stop it,
But someone will destroy,
The rainforest,
I never knew what I was doing.

Gorillas were going extinct,
They can live,
Animals, birds can fly around,
Live in trees,
No animals need to be frightened,
Let the trees, animals and us live.

Jude Brennan (11)
St Michael's RC School, Bermondsey

Pollution, Pollution

Pollution, pollution,
We need a solution,
Don't use the car,
It's not that far.

Pollution, pollution,
We need a solution,
You're hurting the air
And you don't even care.

Pollution, pollution,
We need a solution,
It needs to be minimised,
People should open their eyes,
Don't let it get worse, otherwise
The world will burst.

Pollution, pollution,
We need a solution,
The whale had no fear,
Until pollution came near.

Pollution, pollution, we need a solution.

Michelle Nwaesei (12)
St Michael's RC School, Bermondsey

Climution

Climate change is because of the pollution but
Killing the animals is not the solution,
All the polar ice caps melting are making sea levels rise,
So a flash flood in this country will be no surprise,
There's rain outside but the winds are warm,
This will affect the growth of corn,
So pack your bags and leave before the storm,
If you can understand what I say then stop
The climution every day!

Joshua George (12)
St Michael's RC School, Bermondsey

The Man In The Corner

I walked along the street,
I saw a man who really reeked,
He had bags under his eyes, as if he'd never had a good night's sleep, His
beard was as long as a lion's mane,
His teeth were shattered like a broken picture frame.

His hands were extremely weak, he could barely lift them up,
He looked at himself wondering if he would get any luck,
His bottom was so sore,
He could hardly stand up anymore.

He wore rags for clothes,
His shoes were torn and had fallen apart,
They didn't cover his toes,
He sat there rattling his tin,
Praying his next meal wouldn't come out of the bin.

I walked past him giving sympathy,
I looked into his eyes and saw a symptom of fear,
Hoping happiness was near.

Tina Wetshi (11)
St Michael's RC School, Bermondsey

Street Life

Sitting here outside the train station,
Asking strangers for spare change,
Feeling hungry and shivering with the cold,
The darkness surrounds me like a blanket,
But without the warmth.

Watching people hurrying past pretending they can't see me,
How lucky they are to have somewhere to go,
I feel so ashamed and alone,
The light rain showers me with despair.

Faces in the window of the traffic passing by,
Why can't it be me?
Overflowing with jealousy and misery weighs me down,
Everyone seems to have somewhere they belong but me.

Lydia Salmon (12)
St Michael's RC School, Bermondsey

Poem!

No need for littering,
Just put it in the bin,
It doesn't take Einstein to do such a thing,
To throw litter in the bin.

No need to be rude or nasty to others,
Just be nice to them in a simple way,
'Cause they bring their fathers,
So please be sensible every day.

You find it funny; some kids have nothing to eat,
Or have anything on their feet,
But you should help these kids to have some wheat,
Because it's not fun to see kids having nothing to eat.

Stop pollution cos you're causing global warming,
Stop pollution cos there's too much heat,
There would be a big flood coming in the morning,
Stop pollution because there's no rain to grow wheat.

Cameron Cole (12)
St Michael's RC School, Bermondsey

Recycling!

Recycle, recycle is it so hard?
Not doing it is like giving the world a red card,
Is it hard to put your used bottles in the recycling bin?
Is it so hard to put your newspaper or
Glass bottles in the recycling bin?
Recycle all your rubbish, fat and thin
And put all the leftovers in the bin,
Recycle is something you have to do,
In order to keep our world as good as new,
You might think that what I tell you is drastic,
But I believe it's fantastic!
When you recycle you save a tree,
That means more oxygen for you and me,
Instead of making these things go to waste,
Recycle! And make the world a better place.

Daniel Beckley (11)
St Michael's RC School, Bermondsey

The Rainforest

The rainforest is a multicoloured Heaven on Earth,
Take one step into this paradise and you'll be shocked
With the sights you'll see!
The moment you get there, you'll fall head over heels,
This is what the rainforest is!

The animals in the rainforest are beautiful,
You'll see a tiger in a tree,
A monkey swinging from vine to vine,
Alligators snapping *snap, snap!*
This is what the rainforest is!

The plants you see are magnificent! All different colours,
Brown, red, green, yellow, purple and more,
Great canopies hovering above you giving you shade,
This is what the rainforest is!

This is what I think the rainforest is,
But what do you think it is?

Antonia Krupa (11)
St Michael's RC School, Bermondsey

When . . . ?

When is my next meal?
Is it today, tomorrow or never?
When do I get my education?
I get my education by trying my best and by never giving up.

When is the war going to stop?
It's going to stop when we try to make it stop,
Even when all hope is gone, our dreams will not die.

When is it going to stop mattering about my skin colour?
When you make it stop by sticking to what you believe in.

Being homeless does not mean you have no future,
Having nothing does not mean one day you can have it all,
The colour of my skin does not stop me from being who I am.

Shanice Bedford (11)
St Michael's RC School, Bermondsey

Litter, Litter . . .

Litter, litter, everywhere you go,
We tell you to pick it up but you say no,
Litter, litter, you know it's bad,
Why don't you pick it up and you'll feel glad?
Litter, litter, on the ground,
With no care who is around,
Litter, litter, as I walk on by,
It's such a mess, it makes me sigh,
Litter, litter, why oh why,
A gust of wind makes it fly high,
Litter, litter belongs in the bin,
I wished they realised this is a sin,
The streets are like a bin.

Danni-Lee Brooks (11)
St Michael's RC School, Bermondsey

Homeless Hope

Wandering the streets,
Cold, do you know? I guess not,
I'll tell you all I know, every cold winter's eve,
A man in a white suit comes, he sees almost all homeless people,
And gives them something,
He has travelled the world, but has no money,
He has not sinned and asked for nothing,
I don't know him, they say he stops poverty,
And brings joy to those who have less, he visits all,
When he visits, he lays a kiss on everyone's cheek,
No one has felt him, but has seen him,
His name . . .
Hope!

Isla Williamson (11)
St Michael's RC School, Bermondsey

One Nation, One World, One Race

You can be black, Asian, white or not,
Christian, Muslim, Hindu or Catholic,
African, Irish, Indian or South American,
We're still one nation, one world, one race.

Back in the days when we were separated,
From each other, fighting with a never-ending hatred,
That's all gone now cos,
We're still one nation, one world, one race.

Stop the hating, start the loving,
Stop discriminating, start accepting,
Cos you've gotta know by now that . . .
We're still one nation, one world, one race.

Saskia Bassey (11)
St Michael's RC School, Bermondsey

Recycle, Recycle!

Recycle, recycle please,
Otherwise damage will happen to trees.

So recycle, recycle please,
Save those cute little leaves!

Paper is white like snow,
Surely this you know,
So recycle paper too,
Who knows?
It could come back as part of a shoe,
Recycle, recycle please,
Do you seriously want to damage trees?

Terri Duffin (11)
St Michael's RC School, Bermondsey

The World

Oh world, oh world,
I wish for you to stay,
Oh world, oh world,
You give us so much
But we give you pain,
Oh world, oh world,
Stay with us forever, we are begging you,
Please! Oh world, oh world,
Forgive our selfishness for now and forever!

Diego Casa-Quispe (11)
St Michael's RC School, Bermondsey

A Racism And Recycling Poem

Whenever I see people,
I always see some faces, but it still hurts me,
When I see people being racist,
Some people live in the same house,
Or same estate but still don't want to share.

There are so many people on the Earth that don't care,
I think we should just recycle and not just throw it anywhere.

Recycle, reuse, reduce.

William Polius (11)
St Michael's RC School, Bermondsey

My Favourite Things

R euse everything you can,
E veryone get involved,
C an I make a difference?
Y es I can,
C an you make a difference?
L ots of people can,
E veryone get involved.

Jessica Lee (12)
St Michael's RC School, Bermondsey

The War

I saw the war in Warsaw when I was poor,
Then I saw war dealt with by the law,
A few years later, when I heard the guns no more,
I came out of my door
And therefore I feared the war no more,
The war in Warsaw was knocking upon my door,
Then I found out that the war had been very poor,
When I heard that the law said goodbye to war.

Bobby Apicella (12)
St Michael's RC School, Bermondsey

Recycling

Recycling is like a circle that keeps on going and going,
Recycling is a ball that keeps on rolling,
Recycling has no end.

Kerry Mulvihill (11)
St Michael's RC School, Bermondsey

Responsibility

The heavy gun rested still in my hands.
Gently I stroked the trigger.
For the first time in my life I felt responsible,
Responsible for someone's life.
The moment I squeezed that trigger,
A life would be lost,
A family broken,
A grave to be dug. So simple.
The sergeant stood over me,
Watching me cradle the weapon.
He placed his shaking hand on my shoulder,
Suddenly, his grip tightened,
'Go!' he shouted to us. 'Go!'

Tamsin Woosley (11)
The Arts Educational School, Chiswick

Poor Environment

Pollution, rainforests,
Litter and war,
There has not been
A worse time for
People being poor.

Animals and extinction,
Climate change and racism.

All we have to do is . . .
Recycle, be politer and don't kill for fun.

Think of how much better the world would be
For children growing up.

Eloise Davis (11)
The Arts Educational School, Chiswick

The World

Litter is bitter to the world,
Why not recycle?
Seeing dead animals anywhere is not a pleasant sight,
Just imagine what would happen if that were you?
I love my home but not many people can say the same,
War?
What is war?
Why is there war?
I can hardly breathe with all the pollution,
Why is there pollution?
Think.
Is there not a way to solve anything in life?

Tannika Wilson (13)
The Arts Educational School, Chiswick

Rainforests

To the animals the rainforest is like their protector,
Which is like how we have homes which give us roofs over our heads,
Imagine if someone came to your house and
Knocked it down with a huge bulldozer for no reason,
That's probably how the poor animals feel
When the rainforest gets cut down and
We do not want them to feel like that do we?
So save the rainforests, the animals, the ecosystem
And of course the world.

Sophien Hildebrandt-Petillo (11)
The Arts Educational School, Chiswick

Act Now

Being green isn't a chore,
It won't take much to help more,
Those cans you use, place in the bin,
Leave the next generation something to live in.

The paper, bottles and pieces of can,
All are made by and destroying Man,
It's not just the birds that need a home,
Please think before destroying the ozone.

Share a car or even walk,
Come on, do more than talk,
This world won't last forever, don't think it will,
It can't be solved by a plug or pill.

Being green is not a chore,
It won't take much to help more,
Those cans you use, place in the bin,
Leave something for the next generation to live in!

Holly Motion (17)
West Kent College, Tonbridge

I Am

You look at me like I am nothing,
I am not afraid anymore,
You brought me down until I was lower than low,
I am not she anymore,
The pain, the tears for reasons unknown to others,
That will not happen anymore,
The colours of the rainbow for I was them all,
That will not be me anymore,
Do you feel pleased in what you have achieved?
I do not think so, not anymore,
What was your aim in choosing me? I know I was weak,
I do not think that is too important anymore,
Your ways just made me stronger for now I believe,
I can do anything, but you are no more.

Shanisa Emmons (17)
West Kent College, Tonbridge

Young Writers
Information

We hope you have enjoyed reading this book - and that you will continue to enjoy it in the coming years.

If you like reading and writing poetry drop us a line, or give us a call, and we'll send you a free information pack.

Alternatively if you would like to order further copies of this book or any of our other titles, then please give us a call or log onto our website at www.youngwriters.co.uk

Young Writers Information
Remus House
Coltsfoot Drive
Peterborough
PE2 9JX
(01733) 890066

THURSDAY
NIGHT
TIKI LOUNGE

THURSDAY

52 Drinks

NIGHT

That Bring the Tropics Home

TIKI LOUNGE

BY JENNIFER NEWENS

Library of Congress Cataloging-in-Publication
Data available.
ISBN: 978-1-68555-602-0
Ebook ISBN: 978-1-68555-362-3
Library of Congress Control
Number: 2025945582

Manufactured in China.

Design by Rachel Lopez Metzger.
Edited by Margo Winton Parodi.

Photo credits:
Licensed from Shutterstock.com: all pages,
except for 6-7: iStock.com/Ilona Shorokhova;
p. 126 iStock.com/Anton Dobrea;
pp. 14, 19, 20, 36, 47, 48, 50, 78, 81, 82, 84,
92, 102, 106, 110, 112, 119, 122, 125, 132, 141,
142: Alyson Brown

Special thanks to our friends at Rapa Nui Tiki
in Bend, Oregon, for supplying special props
for the photography.

10 9 8 7 6 5 4 3 2 1

The Collective Book Studio®
Oakland, California
www.thecollectivebook.studio

Page 152 constitutes a continuation
of the copyright page.

To all the bartenders and mixologists that inspired the drinks—cheers to you!

CONTENTS

a tiny bit
about tiki-style drinks ...

Tiki-style drinks and the culture they spawned
began in post–Great Depression America when
bar-goers sought a change from the starkness of
the day in the kitschy, tropical-themed Don the
Beachcomber bar founded by Donn Beach, née
Ernest Gantt, in Southern California. His popular
bar served umbrella-garnished, highly alcoholic,
rum-based tropical drinks. The trend then spread
up the coast to Northern California where "Vic"
Bergeron, founded the equally over-the-top Trader
Vic's in the San Francisco Bay Area. Trader Vic's
eventually expanded to become the first nationally
franchised tiki-style bar. Tiki lounges surged in
popularity throughout the 1950s but all but died
out in the 1960s. A revival by a new wave of serious
mixologists in the 2000s firmed up a place for
these tropical-inspired cocktails on bar menus for
the foreseeable future.

But tiki culture has not been without controversy.
The term "tiki" comes from the Māori, the
Indigenous people of New Zealand, and the word
represents a carved wooden symbol of a god
or ancestor. Some critics believe that tiki bar
owners unfairly borrowed aspects of Oceana
and Caribbean culture for their own profit or
stereotyped and mocked it, or worse. With full

acknowledgment of the cultural appropriation that has happened in the past, for the purposes of this book, we are focusing on the delicious ingredients that make up the drinks, rather than the kitsch.

There are many theories about what a true "tiki drink" should contain. Some say that tiki-style drinks must feature a part each of sweet, sour, and strong (meaning booze). And then there is the dilution factor, which skilled mixologists will add in the form of ice or a flavorful, enhancing liquid. Many bartenders believe there also needs to be a spice component in a tiki-style drink, which is why you often see the addition of cinnamon, nutmeg, and even cloves in drinks offered in a tiki lounge. In this book, I'm keeping it loose, celebrating tropical flavors and strong, mostly rum-based drinks inspired by ingredients from Polynesia and the Caribbean. Though there's a drink for every Thursday of the year, I'm focusing mostly on tropical fruits available year-round; think pineapple, coconut, mango, passion fruit, citrus, banana, and more. As such, the "seasons" of the chapters are tongue-in-cheek nods to a tropical beach vacation in your own home, where the right drink can make it feel like summer all year long.

For each of these recipes, I suggest a glass type, mixing method, and garnish to make the most of the ingredients and make every drink special—even on a Thursday. ENJOY!

a tiny bit about rum…

The majority of tiki-style drinks are built with rum as a base. Broadly speaking, rum is a spirit made from either sugar cane juice or the molasses left over from processing it. The juice or molasses is fermented and then distilled. Rums made from sugarcane juice (such as those made in Martinique, called rhum Agricole) have grassy or herbaceous flavors. Rums made from molasses have rounder flavors and, when aged, exhibit caramel, coffee, and—fittingly—molasses notes.

the six main types of rum used in this book…

LIGHT RUM Light rum is aged in stainless steel containers or briefly aged in wood and filtered before bottling. Light rum is clear in color and mild in flavor. It is usually used as a background spirit for when you want a cohesive cocktail where no ingredient is more pronounced than another.

GOLDEN RUM Golden rum is aged in wood barrels for 1 to 5 years, which gives it its beautiful golden hue. Its flavor seems sweeter than that of light rum, though no sugar is added. The wood selected for aging imparts additional flavors to the liquor, such as coconut, vanilla, nuts, and more.

DARK RUM Dark rum is aged in wood barrels for 3 to 12 years, or even longer for premium rum. It is darker in color and deeper in flavor than golden rum. Like with its younger cousin,

the wood selected to age the dark rum imparts essences in the liquor, and these robust flavors are prized in a variety of tiki-style drinks. Dark rum is often blended with other rum styles to create complex cocktails.

BLACK RUM The darkest rum is called black rum, which is aged in wood barrels for 2 to 5 years, sometimes in barrels that have been heavily charred, contributing to the dark color and strong, smoky-caramelly flavor of the spirit. Some manufacturers of black rum add additional burnt caramel to the blend for extra-strong flavor.

FLAVORED RUM Rum can be flavored with a variety of different spices and fruits. In this book, I use coconut rum—coconut is a classic ingredient in tiki-style cocktails—for a selection of drinks.

OVERPROOF RUM The typical "proof" of spirits available for sale in liquor stores in the United States is 80 to 100 (40 to 50 percent alcohol by volume, or ABV). For rum in particular, if the ABV exceeds 40 to 50 percent, it is labeled "overproof." Overproof rum appears frequently in tiki-style drinks, as they have a reputation for being unabashedly boozy. In this book, several drinks call for 151-proof rum, often as a float on top of the drink, and it's often optional if you don't want to go overboard.

a tiny bit about barware ...

Cocktail shaker There are two common types of shakers: cobbler and Boston. A cobbler shaker includes a cup basin with a detachable top, measuring cap, and strainer. A Boston shaker uses two weighted, metal cups that seal together to quickly mix multiple drinks.

Mixing glass As the older sibling to the cocktail shaker, the mixing glass serves a similar purpose, though it generally produces a less-diluted cocktail. A mixing glass requires the use of a strainer and a barspoon.

Strainer The most common strainer is the Hawthorne strainer, which is all you'll need for most cocktails. If you want a finer strain, such as when you are using seedy berries, you can use a fine-mesh sieve.

Barspoon While any spoon will technically work for mixing a cocktail, the traditional barspoon has an extra-long handle to keep the bartender's fingers away from the drink and give extra mobility when stirring.

Jigger or measured shot glass A jigger is a liquid measuring tool designed specifically for cocktail mixing. It notes common measurements and comes in several sizes.

Citrus press The drinks in this book recommend the use of fresh citrus juice whenever possible. A handheld citrus press is an easy-to-use and nearly irreplaceable tool when extracting fresh lime or lemon juice at home. A larger citrus juicer is helpful for orange and grapefruit juice.

Muddler A muddler is a simple wooden or metal tool resembling a miniature baseball bat with a long handle and flat bottom. It works to mash ingredients to express their flavors and aromas before adding the liquids for cocktails.

High-speed blender Many tiki-style drinks call for serving over crushed ice or are blended with ice to create a slushy texture. I highly recommend a high-speed blender for the job. High-speed blenders have more power than regular blenders to crush ice and create a more uniform texture in your special drinks. This category of blenders tends to be pricier than a standard blender model, but I've found the investment is worth it for their reliability and versatility beyond just cocktails.

a tiny bit about glassware …

Cocktail glasses come in all shapes and sizes. While each recipe suggests an appropriate type of glassware, the real star of the show will always be the drink itself. Below is a list of the glassware used in this book, but you can pour your tiki-style cocktail into any vessel you choose.

Coupe	Highball	Old fashioned
Coffee mug	Hurricane	Double old fashioned
Champagne flute	Margarita	Tiki mug
	Martini	

EARLY SUMMER

NAVY GROG

Here's a simple cocktail made famous at Los Angeles's Don the Beachcomber restaurants. Rum was historically a favorite of the British Royal Navy. As with many tiki-style cocktails, a blend of rums is called for. Use this as a template for discovering your own favorite types of rum and blending them into a complex elixir that suits your own personal tastes.

GLASS: Double old fashioned	GARNISH: Citrus wedge and mint sprig
1 oz/30 ml light rum 1 oz/30 ml golden rum 1 oz/30 ml dark rum ¾ oz/22 ml fresh lime juice ¾ oz/22 ml fresh grapefruit juice	¼ oz/7 ml Honey Syrup (see Tip, page 41) ¼ oz/7 ml allspice dram (see Tip, page 129) Sparkling water Citrus wedge, for garnish Mint sprig, for garnish

In a cocktail shaker, add the light rum, golden rum, dark rum, lime juice, grapefruit juice, honey syrup, and allspice dram. Add ice and shake until chilled. Strain into a cocktail glass over ice cubes or crushed ice and top with sparkling water. Garnish with a citrus wedge and mint sprig. Makes 1 cocktail.

DEMERARA DRY FLOAT

Tiki-style cocktail king Don the Beachcomber invented this cocktail, which records show he came up with in the early 1940s. It has seen a bit of a renaissance in recent years. True to the genre, the drink is boozy, complex, fruity, and goes down easy.

GLASS: Double old fashioned	GARNISH: Lime wheel
2 oz/60 ml dark rum, preferably Demerara 1½ oz/45 ml fresh lime juice 1½ oz/45 ml passion fruit syrup	¼ oz/7 ml Simple Syrup (see Tip, page 62) ¼ oz/7 ml maraschino liqueur ½ oz/15 ml 151-proof rum Lime wheel, for garnish

In a cocktail shaker, add the dark rum, lime juice, passion fruit syrup, simple syrup, and maraschino liqueur. Add ice and shake until chilled. Strain into a cocktail glass over ice. Carefully pour the 151-proof rum over the back of a barspoon into the glass to float on top. Garnish with a lime wheel. Makes 1 cocktail.

TRADEWINDS

Depending on the source, Tradewinds recipes call for
different types of rum, from Jamaican to golden to
black to "lightly aged" or even specific brands. My
advice: Experiment with two different rums you like,
aiming for contrasting characteristics that, when
layered together, make you smile. Bartenders often
turn the paper umbrella inside out when garnishing
this cocktail as a whimsical nod to the drink's name.

GLASS: Highball	GARNISH: Pineapple fronds and paper umbrella

1½ oz/45 ml fresh lemon juice

1 oz/30 ml dark rum

1 oz/30 ml light rum

1 oz/30 ml Homemade Cream of Coconut (see Tip, page 29)

½ oz/15 ml apricot or peach liqueur

Pineapple fronds, for garnish

Paper umbrella, for garnish

In a cocktail shaker, add the lemon juice, dark rum, light rum,
cream of coconut, and apricot liqueur. Add ice and shake
until chilled. Strain into a chilled cocktail glass over crushed
ice and garnish with pineapple fronds and a paper umbrella.
Makes 1 cocktail.

RUM RUNNER

This sweet-tart, punch-like cocktail is delicious for when you want a refreshing, fruit-forward sip. My research reveals that it was likely invented in the Florida Keys, some say by a bartender who was trying to use up a bunch of excess ingredients.

GLASS: Hurricane or highball	GARNISH: Pineapple wedge, pineapple frond, and cocktail cherry
1 oz/30 ml pineapple juice	½ oz/15 ml Homemade Grenadine (see Tip, page 25)
1 oz/30 ml fresh lime juice	Pineapple frond, for garnish
1 oz/30 ml banana liqueur	Pineapple wedge, for garnish
1 oz/30 ml Chambord	Cocktail cherry, for garnish
¾ oz/22 ml dark rum	
¾ oz/22 ml light rum	

In a cocktail shaker, add the pineapple juice, lime juice, banana liqueur, Chambord, dark and light rums, and grenadine. Add ice and shake until chilled. Strain into a cocktail glass over ice. Garnish with a pineapple wedge, pineapple frond, and cocktail cherry. Makes 1 cocktail.

Homemade Grenadine

In a saucepan, combine 2 cups/
475 ml unsweetened pomegranate juice,
2 cups/400 g sugar, and 1 oz/30 ml fresh
lemon juice. Warm over medium heat
until the sugar is completely dissolved;
take care not to boil the mixture.
Remove from the heat and
cool completely, then stir in 1 or
2 dashes orange flower water.
Makes about 3 cups/700 ml.

PAINKILLER

This cocktail was created in the early 1970s at the Soggy Dollar Bar in the British Virgin Islands. For an authentic drink, use Pusser's rum, an aged spirit blended to the specifications of the British Royal Navy and the rum of choice for use in this drink at the Soggy Dollar.

GLASS: Hurricane or highball	GARNISH: Pineapple wedge and pineapple fronds

3 oz/90 ml pineapple juice

2 oz/60 ml dark rum

1 oz/30 ml Homemade Cream of Coconut (see Tip, page 29)

1 oz/30 ml fresh orange juice

Pineapple wedge, for garnish

In a cocktail shaker, add the pineapple juice, rum, cream of coconut, and orange juice. Add ice and shake until chilled. Strain into a cocktail glass over crushed ice. Garnish with a pineapple wedge and pineapple fronds. Makes 1 cocktail.

Homemade Cream of Coconut

In a saucepan, combine 1 can (13.5 oz/
380 ml) unsweetened full-fat coconut
milk, 1½ cups/300 g sugar, and a pinch
of kosher salt. Place over medium-low
heat and warm until the sugar dissolves
and the mixture is smooth, about
3 minutes. Stir in 1 tablespoon coconut
milk powder and, using an immersion
blender, blend until smooth and no
lumps remain. Let cool completely,
then transfer to a jar and refrigerate
until ready to use.
Makes 2¼ to 2½ cups/530 to 590 ml.

JUNGLE BIRD

The bright orange Campari in this cocktail gives it a beautiful hue, just like a showy bird in the tropics. The origin of this drink is said to be from the now closed Kuala Lumpur Hilton in the 1970s.

GLASS: Old fashioned	GARNISH: Pineapple chunks

2 oz/60 ml pineapple juice
1¾ oz/52 ml black rum
¾ oz/22 ml fresh lime juice
¾ oz/22 ml Campari
½ oz/15 ml Simple Syrup (see Tip, page 62)
Pineapple chunks, for garnish

In a cocktail shaker, add the pineapple juice, rum, lime juice, Campari, and simple syrup. Add ice and shake until chilled. Strain into a cocktail glass over ice. Garnish with pineapple chunks. Makes 1 cocktail.

PERSONEATER

Here is my take on a Maneater cocktail, a drink I found on a website called Taste & Tipple. I was intrigued by this one, as it was gin-based instead of rum-based, and I had fun playing with pairing typical ingredients in the tropical cocktail catalog in a different way.

GLASS: Tiki mug or highball	GARNISH: Pineapple wedge, pineapple fronds, and edible flower

2 oz/60 ml pineapple juice	½ oz/15 ml orange Curaçao
1½ oz/45 ml gin	¼ oz/7 ml Star Anise Simple Syrup (see Tip, page 63)
¾ oz/22 ml fresh lime juice	Pineapple fronds, for garnish
¾ oz/22 ml Homemade Orgeat (see Tip, page 45)	Pineapple wedge, for garnish
½ oz/15 ml peach liqueur	Edible flower, for garnish

In a cocktail shaker, add the pineapple juice, gin, lime juice, orgeat, peach liqueur, Curaçao, and simple syrup. Add ice and shake until chilled. Strain into a cocktail glass over crushed ice and garnish with a pineapple wedge, pineapple fronds, and an edible flower. Makes 1 cocktail.

CLASSIC DAIQUIRI

The classic daiquiri is refreshing, simple, and lacks the typical long ingredient list and high-proof punch of what is typically seen on a tiki lounge menu. Adjust the flavor to your liking by trying different flavors of simple syrup.

GLASS: Coupe or Martini	GARNISH: Lime twist

2 oz/60 ml light rum

1¼ oz/37 ml fresh lime juice

¾ oz/22 ml Simple Syrup (see Tip, page 62)

Lime twist, for garnish

In a cocktail shaker, add the rum, lime juice, and simple syrup. Add ice and shake until chilled. Strain into a chilled cocktail glass and garnish with a lime twist. Makes 1 cocktail.

MOORÉA SUNSET

When I was reminiscing about a trip to Mooréa, an island near Tahiti, two memories stood out: fresh mango juice in the lobby upon arrival and visiting a vanilla orchid farm to experience how the exotic ingredient was grown. For this drink, I combined the two—mango juice and vanilla in the form of vanilla-infused simple syrup—into an original cocktail inspired by that memorable vacation.

GLASS: Old fashioned	GARNISH: Lime wheel
2 oz/60 ml mango juice 2 oz/60 ml light rum ½ oz/15 ml fresh lime juice ½ oz/15 ml Vanilla Simple Syrup (see Tip, page 63)	½ oz/15 ml Homemade Grenadine (see Tip, page 25) Lime wheel, for garnish

In a cocktail shaker, add the mango juice, rum, lime juice, simple syrup, and grenadine. Add ice and shake until chilled. Strain into a cocktail glass over ice and garnish with a lime wheel. Makes 1 cocktail.

THREE DOTS AND A DASH

|

The name of this classic cocktail is morse code for the letter "V," alluding to the Allied victory in World War II. Legend has it that Donn Beach created this drink during that era as a commemoration of the event. I prefer Amarena cherries to maraschino for this cocktail . . . plus, I had an open jar in my fridge.

GLASS: Highball	GARNISH: 3 cocktail cherries and pineapple fronds
1½ oz/45 ml golden rum, preferably rhum Agricole	¼ oz/7 ml falernum syrup, (see Tip, page 101)
½ oz/15 ml light rum	¼ oz/7 ml allspice dram (see Tip, page 129)
½ oz/15 ml fresh lime juice	
½ oz/15 ml fresh orange juice	Dash of Angostura bitters
½ oz/15 ml Honey Syrup (see Tip, page 41)	Pineapple fronds, for garnish
	3 cocktail cherries, for garnish

In a cocktail shaker, add the golden rum, light rum, lime juice, orange juice, honey syrup, falernum syrup, allspice dram, and bitters. Add ice and shake until chilled. Strain into a cocktail glass over crushed ice and garnish with 3 cherries threaded on a skewer and a few pineapple fronds. Makes 1 cocktail.

Honey Syrup

Combine ½ cup/120 ml local honey with ½ cup/120 ml water in a small saucepan. Warm over medium heat, stirring constantly, until the honey is dissolved. Take care that the mixture does not boil. Remove from the heat. Let cool completely, then store in an airtight container in the refrigerator until ready to use. Makes about 1 cup /240 ml.

HAWAIIAN SUNSET

Made popular in the now-closed Aku Aku Polynesian restaurant in Las Vegas's Stardust Hotel, this cocktail is a rarity in the tiki-style canon for its use of vodka instead of rum. The grenadine gives it a gorgeous pink color, which lends the drink its name.

GLASS: Coupe	GARNISH: Dried Lime wheel

2 oz/60 ml vodka

½ oz/15 ml Homemade Orgeat (see Tip, page 45)

½ oz/15 ml fresh lime juice

½ oz/15 ml fresh lemon juice

Splash of Homemade Grenadine (see Tip, page 25)

Dried lime wheel, for garnish

In a cocktail shaker, add the vodka, orgeat, lime juice, lemon juice, and grenadine. Add ice and shake until chilled. Strain into a cocktail glass and garnish with a dried lime wheel. Makes 1 cocktail.

Homemade Orgeat

In a food processor, pulse 2 cups/300 g
blanched slivered almonds until finely
ground. In a saucepan over medium heat,
bring 1 cup/240 ml Turbinado Syrup
(see Tip, page 75) to a simmer. Add the
ground almonds and return to a simmer.
Reduce the heat to low and simmer
for 3 minutes. Slowly increase the
temperature to medium-high. Just before
the mixture starts to boil, remove the pan
from the heat and cover it with a lid.
Let stand for 3 to 8 hours, then strain
through two layers of cheesecloth. Stir in
1 oz/30 ml vodka, 1 teaspoon orange-
flower water, and 1 teaspoon almond
extract. Transfer the orgeat to a jar and
store in the refrigerator for up to 2 weeks.
Makes 1 to 1¼ cups (240 to 300 ml)

SINGAPORE SLING

Many aficionados wouldn't consider this a true tiki-style drink because of its Asian roots—it was invented at the Raffles Hotel in Singapore in 1915—and lack of rum. But its tropical and citrus fruit juices, bold spirit base, and layered, spice-laden formula will still thrill tiki enthusiasts, warranting its inclusion here as a compelling outlier.

GLASS: Hurricane	GARNISH: Orange wedge and cocktail cherry
1 oz/30 ml pineapple juice	2 dashes Angostura bitters
¾ oz/22 ml gin	Sparkling water
½ oz/15 ml fresh lime juice	Orange wedge, for garnish
¼ oz/7 ml brandy	Cocktail cherry, for garnish
¼ oz/7 ml orange Curaçao	
¼ oz/7 ml maraschino liqueur	

In a cocktail shaker, add the pineapple juice, gin, lime juice, brandy, Curaçao, maraschino liqueur, and bitters. Add ice and shake until chilled. Strain into a cocktail glass over ice. Top with the sparkling water. Garnish with an orange wedge and cocktail cherry. Makes 1 cocktail.

BEACHCOMBER

Given its name, you would think this drink would be one of Donn Beach's specialties, but actually it was popularized by Vic Bergeron at Trader Vic's. Some consider this to be in the daiquiri family of cocktails. Here, it's blended with ice and served in a pleasing slushy format. You can also shake the ingredients in a cocktail shaker and serve it up (with the ice strained).

GLASS: Martini	GARNISH: Cocktail cherry

4 oz/120 ml light rum

1½ oz/45 ml orange Curaçao

1½ oz/45 ml fresh lime juice

½ oz/15 ml maraschino liqueur

1 cup/150 g ice cubes

2 cocktail cherries, for garnish

In a high-speed blender, add the rum, curaçao, lime juice, maraschino liqueur, and ice and blend until smooth.
Pour into a cocktail glass. Garnish with a cocktail cherry.
Makes 2 cocktails.

SUMMER

MODERN AKU AKU

Here's a new interpretation of a classic cocktail invented at Trader Vic's restaurant. The proprietor, Vic Bergeron, borrowed heavily from Polynesian culture to name his drinks; to wit, "Aku Aku" refers to "spirit" in Easter Island mythology. (Though rum was not the spirit the Rapa Nui were referring to.) The original drink was blended with ice to make a slushy concoction. Here, I treat it like a mojito and muddle the mint first, then add the remaining ingredients and serve it over ice.

GLASS: Highball	GARNISH: Mint sprig and lime half-wheel

Small handful fresh mint leaves

1½ oz/45 ml pineapple juice

1 oz/30 ml light rum

¾ oz/22 ml fresh lime juice

½ oz/15 ml peach liqueur

½ oz/15 ml Turbinado Syrup (see Tip, page 75)

Sparkling water

Mint sprig, for garnish

Lime slice, for garnish

In a cocktail glass, muddle the mint. Add the pineapple juice, rum, lime juice, peach liqueur, and turbinado syrup. Fill the glass with ice. Top with sparkling water. Garnish with a mint sprig and lime half-wheel. Makes 1 cocktail.

LAVA FLOW

*This drink, with its two distinct blended layers
that melt and flow together like lava into earth,
may remind you of a blend of a piña colada
and a frozen strawberry daiquiri. Try one on
a warm evening when you feel indecisive.*

GLASS: Hurricane		GARNISH: Pineapple wedge

20 fresh strawberries

2 oz/60 ml golden rum

1 cup/150 g ice cubes

⅔ ripe banana, peeled and
cut into chunks

2 oz/60 ml Homemade
Cream of Coconut (see Tip,
page 29)

2 oz/60 ml pineapple juice

2 oz/60 ml coconut rum

2 pineapple wedges,
for garnish

In a high-speed blender, combine the strawberries, golden
rum, and half of the ice cubes. Blend until smooth, then
divide between 2 cocktail glasses. Rinse the blender.

Add the banana, cream of coconut, pineapple juice, coconut
rum, and remaining ice cubes to the blender and blend until
smooth. Pour into the glasses on top of the strawberry
mixture. Garnish with a pineapple wedge. Makes 2 cocktails.

BLUE HAWAIIAN

This blue-hued drink evokes the color of a swimming pool, and on a hot day, what could be better? It has similar ingredients to a piña colada, but it is shaken instead of blended.

GLASS: Double old fashioned or hurricane	GARNISH: Cocktail cherry and pineapple wedge
2 oz/60 ml light rum	½ oz/15 ml fresh lime juice
1½ oz/45 ml pineapple juice	Cocktail cherry, for garnish
¾ oz/22 ml blue Curaçao	Pineapple wedge, for garnish
¾ oz/22 ml Homemade Cream of Coconut (see Tip, page 29)	

In a cocktail shaker, add the rum, pineapple juice, Curaçao, cream of coconut, and lime juice. Add ice and shake until chilled. Strain into a cocktail glass over ice. Garnish with a cocktail cherry and pineapple wedge. Makes 1 cocktail.

COCONUT MOJITO

Some might argue that a mojito is not a proper tiki-style drink, but for the purposes of this book, I think it fits: It features flavors from the tropics, it's refreshing on a hot day, and it looks great next to a book poolside. That it is not high in alcohol and does not require a long list of ingredients? I'll still give it a pass. For this version, I've used coconut rum for an extra taste of the tropics.

GLASS: Highball	GARNISH: Mint leaves and lime wedges
8 fresh mint leaves, plus more for garnish	Sparkling water
2 oz/60 ml coconut rum	Lime wedges, for garnish
2 oz/60 ml fresh lime juice	
½ oz/15 ml Simple Syrup (see Tip, page 62), or more to taste	

In a cocktail glass, muddle the mint. Add the rum, lime juice, and simple syrup and stir. Fill the glass with ice, then top with sparkling water. Garnish with mint leaves and lime wedges. Makes 1 cocktail.

SPICED PIÑA COLADA

In researching this book, I discovered that some cocktail scholars believe that true tiki-style drinks should have a component of spice in their formula. That got me curious to see if a spiced simple syrup in a piña colada recipe would be successful. I was pleasantly surprised, and this recipe was born. For a standard piña colada, swap out the star anise simple syrup for regular simple syrup.

GLASS: Highball	GARNISH: Pineapple wedge
2 cups/300 g fresh or frozen pineapple chunks 1 cup/150 grams ice cubes Cream from 1 can (13.5 oz/ 380 ml) unsweetened full-fat coconut milk (reserve milk for another use)	4 oz/120 ml light rum 1 oz/30 ml fresh lime juice ¼ oz/7 ml Star Anise Simple Syrup (see Tip, page 63) 2 pineapple slices, for garnish

In a high-speed blender, add the pineapple, ice cubes, the coconut cream, rum, lime juice, and star anise simple syrup. Blend until smooth and frosty. Pour into 2 cocktail glasses. Garnish each with a pineapple wedge. Makes 2 cocktails.

TIP

Simple Syrup

Combine 1 cup/200 g granulated sugar with 1 cup water in a small saucepan. Bring to a boil, then lower the heat and simmer, stirring occasionally, until the sugar is dissolved, about 10 minutes. Cool completely, then store in an airtight container in the refrigerator for up to 2 weeks. Makes 1½ cups/350 ml.

Cinnamon Simple Syrup

Add 2 cinnamon sticks, broken in half, to the pan with the hot simple syrup. Let stand at room temperature for at least 2 hours, preferably overnight, before using.

Star Anise Simple Syrup

Add 4 whole star anise to the pan with the hot simple syrup. Let stand at room temperature for at least 2 hours, preferably overnight, before using.

Vanilla Simple Syrup

Add 1 vanilla bean, split lengthwise, to the pan with the hot simple syrup. Let stand at room temperature for at least 2 hours, preferably overnight, before using.

CHI CHI

Another invention of Donn Beach, the Chi Chi is essentially a piña colada spiked with vodka instead of rum. If you like, experiment with flavored vodkas to create different versions, depending on your mood.

GLASS: Highball	GARNISH: Pineapple wedges

4 oz/120 ml vodka

4 oz/120 ml pineapple juice

1½ oz/45 ml Homemade Cream of Coconut (see Tip, page 29)

¾ oz/22 ml fresh lime juice

2 cups/300 g ice cubes

2 pineapple slices for garnish

In a high-speed blender, add the vodka, pineapple juice, cream of coconut, lime juice, and ice cubes. Blend until smooth and frosty. Divide between 2 cocktail glasses. Garnish each with pineapple wedges. Makes 2 cocktails.

FROZEN STRAWBERRY DAIQUIRI

I like to spike my daiquiri with a little coconut rum and, for a change of pace, some fresh herbs. During strawberry season, arrange fresh hulled strawberries in a single layer on a rimmed baking sheet and place it in the freezer until frozen, 1 to 2 hours. When frozen, transfer to a locking freezer bag for future use.

GLASS: Margarita	GARNISH: Fresh strawberry
2 cups/300 g frozen strawberries	10 leaves fresh mint or basil, chopped (optional)
3 oz/90 ml light rum	1 cup/150 g ice cubes
1 oz/30 ml coconut rum	Fresh strawberries, for garnish
¾ oz/22 ml fresh lime juice	
½ oz/15 ml Simple Syrup (see Tip, page 62), or to taste	

In a high-speed blender, add the frozen berries, light rum, coconut rum, lime juice, simple syrup, mint, if using, and ice cubes and blend until smooth. Divide between 2 cocktail glasses. Garnish each with a fresh strawberry. Makes 2 cocktails.

SPICED SEX ON THE BEACH

A Sex on the Beach is not normally considered a tiki-style drink, but the drink does have the word "beach" in it, right? Here, I've modified the cocktail to include more of the elements you might find in a tiki lounge drink—rum, pomegranate (a component of grenadine), and spice—for a sultry sip on a warm night.

GLASS: Hurricane	GARNISH: Cocktail cherry

1 oz/30 ml fresh orange juice

1 oz/30 ml unsweetened pomegranate juice

1 oz/30 ml vodka

1 oz/30 ml light rum

½ oz/15 ml peach liqueur

¼ oz/7 ml Cinnamon Simple Syrup (see Tip, page 63)

Cocktail cherry, for garnish

In a cocktail shaker, add the orange juice, pomegranate juice, vodka, rum, peach liqueur, and simple syrup. Add ice and shake until chilled. Strain into a cocktail glass over crushed ice. Garnish with a cocktail cherry. Makes 1 cocktail.

MISSIONARY'S DOWNFALL

*This gorgeous green cocktail was a product
of Don the Beachcomber's bar in Los Angeles
circa the late 1930s. One can only guess about the
cocktail's name, but after testing this recipe,
I can confirm that it would be easy to down
a few without realizing how strong they are.*

GLASS: Highball	GARNISH: Mint sprig and pineapple wedge
1 cup/150 g fresh pineapple chunks	10 large fresh mint leaves, torn
4 oz/120 ml light rum	2 cups/300 g ice cubes
1½ oz/45 ml fresh lime juice	2 mint sprigs, for garnish
1 oz/30 ml peach liqueur	2 pineapple wedges, for garnish
1 oz/30 ml Honey Syrup (see Tip, page 41)	

In a high-speed blender, combine the pineapple, rum,
lime juice, peach liqueur, honey syrup, mint, and ice cubes.
Blend until smooth, then divide between 2 cocktail glasses.
Garnish each with a mint sprig and pineapple wedge.
Makes 2 cocktails.

BANANA COW

|

In the 1970s, "Trader Vic" Bergeron claimed that this was the best hangover cure a bartender could serve, better even than a Bloody Mary. While modern medicine may credit the potassium in the bananas, not the recipe itself, for any curative effects, the important thing is that this makes a great cocktail, whether you're enjoying it in the evening or "recovering" the next day.

GLASS: Highball	GARNISH: Banana slice

1 very ripe banana, peeled and cut into chunks

6 oz/180 ml whole milk

4 oz/120 ml golden rum

1½ oz/45 ml Turbinado Syrup (see Tip, page 75)

2 dashes Angostura bitters

1 cup/150 g ice cubes

2 banana slices, for garnish

In a blender, combine the bananas, milk, rum, turbinado syrup, bitters, and ice cubes. Blend until smooth, then divide between 2 cocktail glasses. Garnish each with a banana slice. Makes 2 cocktails.

Turbinado Syrup

In many tiki lounges, bartenders use demerara syrup, but turbinado sugar is easier to find than demerara sugar, and the flavor is similar.

Combine 2 cups/400 g turbinado sugar with 8 oz/240 ml water in a small saucepan. Bring to a boil and simmer, stirring occasionally, until the sugar is dissolved, about 10 minutes. Cool completely, then store in an airtight container. Makes 2 cups/475 ml.

ANCIENT MARINER

Originally created by Jeff "Beachbum" Berry, a New Orleans restaurateur, this smoky, spicy cocktail is on the simpler side of the tiki-style cocktail catalog. For authenticity, use half Demerara rum (a rum made exclusively in Guyana) and half Jamaican rum.

GLASS: Tiki mug or old fashioned	GARNISH: Grapefruit wedge and cocktail cherry

2 oz/60 ml dark rum

¾ oz/22 ml fresh lime juice

¾ oz/22 ml fresh grapefruit juice

½ oz/15 ml Simple Syrup (see Tip, page 62)

¼ oz/7 ml allspice dram (see Tip, page 129)

Grapefruit wedge, for garnish

Cocktail cherry, for garnish

In a cocktail shaker, add the rum, lime juice, grapefruit juice, simple syrup, and allspice dram. Add ice and shake until chilled. Strain into a cocktail glass over crushed ice and garnish with a grapefruit wedge and cocktail cherry. Makes 1 cocktail.

TEST PILOT

There are multiple versions of this recipe in the cocktail universe, though most believe it to be an invention of Donn Beach. The Pernod gives it just a hint of anise spice.

GLASS: Tiki mug or old fashioned	GARNISH: Lime wedge

1½ oz/45 ml dark rum

¾ oz/22 ml light rum

½ oz/15 ml fresh lime juice

¼ oz/7 ml falernum syrup (see Tip, page 101)

¼ oz/7 ml orange Curaçao

Splash of Pernod

Dash of Angostura bitters

Lime wedge, for garnish

In a cocktail shaker, add the dark rum, light rum, lime juice, falernum syrup, Curaçao, Pernod, and bitters. Add ice and shake until chilled. Strain into a cocktail glass over ice cubes or crushed ice and garnish with a lime wedge. Makes 1 cocktail.

FAT SAILOR

The origin of this tiki-style cocktail is hard to discern, but it certainly earns a badge for potency, as many drinks in this category do. I was surprised how well the lime juice offset the coffee flavor of the Kahlúa.

GLASS: Old fashioned	GARNISH: Edible flower and lime wedge

1½ oz/45 ml light rum

1 oz/30 ml fresh lime juice

½ oz/15 ml 151-proof rum

½ oz/15 ml Kahlúa

½ oz/15 ml Simple Syrup (see Tip, page 62)

Edible flower, for garnish

Lime wedge, for garnish

In a cocktail shaker, add the light rum, lime juice, 151-proof rum, Kahlúa, and simple syrup. Add ice and shake until chilled. Strain into a cocktail glass over crushed ice. Garnish with an edible flower and lime wedge. Makes 1 cocktail.

KATE'S MAI TAI

Rumored to have been invented by Vic Bergeron in his Oakland, California, restaurant, Trader Vic's, the Mai Tai is an iconic drink on a tiki lounge menu. This version was created by my long-time hair stylist, Kate, who gave me permission to feature her rendition in the book.

GLASS: Double old fashioned	GARNISH: Lime shell and mint sprig
1 oz/30 ml golden rum, preferably rhum Agricole	¼ oz/7 ml Simple Syrup (see Tip, page 62)
1 oz/30 ml dark rum, preferably Jamaican	½ oz/15 ml 151-proof rum (optional)
1 oz/30 ml fresh lime juice	Lime shell, for garnish
½ oz/15 ml orange Curaçao	Mint sprig, for garnish
¼ oz/7 ml Homemade Orgeat (see Tip, page 45)	

In a cocktail shaker, add the golden rum, dark rum, lime juice, Curaçao, orgeat, and simple syrup. Add ice and shake until chilled. Strain into a cocktail glass over ice cubes. Carefully pour the 151-proof rum, if using, over the back of a barspoon into the glass so that it floats on the top of the drink. Garnish with a lime shell and mint sprig. Makes 1 cocktail.

ZOMBIE

Featuring three different rums, the Zombie earned legendary status at Don the Beachcomber's bar in the 1930s. At that time, customers were limited to just a few drinks due to their potency—perhaps that added to the drink's mystique? The Zombie was exposed to a wider audience when a version was served at the 1939 World's Fair in New York.

GLASS: Tiki mug or highball	GARNISH: Mint sprig
1 oz/30 ml dark rum 1 oz/30 ml golden rum 1 oz/30 ml pineapple juice ¾ oz/22 ml fresh lime juice	½ oz/15 ml Simple Syrup (see Tip, page 62) Splash of Pernod ½ oz/15 ml 151-proof rum Mint sprig, for garnish

In a cocktail shaker, add the dark rum, golden rum, pineapple juice, lime juice, simple syrup, and Pernod. Add ice and shake until chilled. Strain into a cocktail glass over ice. Carefully pour the 151-proof rum over the back of a barspoon into the glass so that it floats on top of the drink. Garnish with a mint sprig. Makes 1 cocktail.

SAFE HARBOR

The components of this simple cocktail might seem familiar, as they are the same as in a Dark 'n Stormy®. But to call it that, you must use Goslings Rum, a rum made in Bermuda, as they hold the trademark on the name.

GLASS: Highball	GARNISH: Dried lime wheels

2 oz/60 ml black rum

1 oz/30 ml fresh lime juice

Dash of Angostura bitters

Chilled ginger beer

Dried lime wheels, for garnish

Fill a cocktail glass with ice and add the rum, lime juice, and bitters. Top with the ginger beer. Garnish with lime wheels. Makes 1 cocktail.

FOG CUTTER

Here's another drink made famous by Vic Bergeron at his Trader Vic's restaurants. In classic tiki style, it uses several different types of spirits to achieve its complex flavor. The sherry is classic, but it can be omitted if desired.

GLASS: Highball	GARNISH: Mint sprig
1 oz/30 ml light rum	½ oz/15 ml gin
1 oz/30 ml fresh orange juice	½ oz/15 ml brandy
1 oz/30 ml fresh lemon juice	½ oz/15 ml amontillado sherry (optional)
½ oz/15 ml orange Curaçao	Mint sprig, for garnish
½ oz/15 ml Homemade Orgeat (see Tip, page 45)	

In a cocktail shaker, add the rum, orange juice, lemon juice, Curaçao, orgeat, gin, and brandy. Add ice and shake until chilled. Strain into a cocktail glass over ice. Carefully pour the sherry, if using, over the back of a barspoon into the glass to float on top of the drink. Garnish with a mint sprig. Makes 1 cocktail.

SCORPION

Here is a scaled-down version of the potent, often shared drink, customized for the Covid era. If you want to serve it the traditional way, in a shared bowl with straws, see the variation below.

GLASS: Highball or tiki mug	GARNISH: Paper umbrella and edible flower
2 oz/60 ml dark rum	½ oz/15 ml brandy
1½ oz/45 ml Homemade Orgeat (see Tip, page 45)	½ oz/15 ml gin
1 oz/30 ml fresh lemon juice	Paper umbrella, for garnish
1 oz/30 ml fresh orange juice	Edible flower, for garnish

In a cocktail shaker, add the rum, orgeat, lemon juice, orange juice, brandy, and gin. Add ice and shake until chilled. Strain into a cocktail glass over crushed ice. Garnish with a paper umbrella and edible flower. Makes 1 cocktail.

VARIATION: **SCORPION BOWL.** *Multiply the quantities of ingredients by 4 and add them to a high-speed blender with 3 cups/450 g ice cubes. Blend until slushy. Pour into a small punchbowl. Garnish with citrus wheels, pineapple fronds, edible flowers, and a paper umbrella and set out 4 long, colorful straws. Makes 4 cocktails.*

BAHAMA MAMA

|

Like many tiki-style cocktails, the origins of the Bahama Mama are shrouded in uncertainty. For our purposes, it is a coffee-inflected, rum-based pineapple drink that tastes amazing and looks great garnished with a juicy slice of fresh pineapple. It's one of the easier cocktails to make, so I like to serve it at a warm-weather get-together.

GLASS: Highball or hurricane	GARNISH: Pineapple wedge and cocktail cherry

2 oz/60 ml pineapple juice

1 oz/30 ml coconut rum

1 oz/30 ml dark rum, preferably overproof

½ oz/15 ml fresh lemon juice

½ oz/15 ml Kahlúa

Pineapple wedge, for garnish

Cocktail cherry for garnish

In a cocktail shaker, add the pineapple juice, coconut rum, dark rum, lemon juice, and Kahlúa. Add ice and shake until chilled. Strain into a cocktail glass over ice. Garnish with a pineapple wedge and cocktail cherry. Makes 1 cocktail.

PLANTER'S PUNCH

The origins of Planter's Punch are hard to pin down, and so is an accurate recipe. But whether or not this formula is authentic, on a hot day, I love the straightforward mix of rum, pineapple juice, and citrus with a splash of homemade grenadine— something I keep on hand all summer long for refreshing, crowd-pleasing cocktails like this one.

GLASS: Hurricane	GARNISH: Pineapple wedge, pineapple frond, and cocktail cherry

2 oz/60 ml dark rum

1 oz/30 ml pineapple juice

1 oz/30 ml fresh orange juice

½ oz/15 ml fresh lime juice

½ oz/15 ml orange Curaçao

½ oz/15 ml Homemade Grenadine (see Tip, page 25)

Pineapple wedge, for garnish

Cocktail cherry, for garnish

In a cocktail shaker, add the rum, pineapple juice, orange juice, lime juice, Curaçao, and grenadine. Add ice and shake until chilled. Strain into a cocktail glass over ice. Garnish with a pineapple wedge, pineapple frond, and cocktail cherry. Makes 1 cocktail.

COBRA'S FANG

|

This cocktail was an early invention of tiki bar pioneer Donn Beach in the late 1930s. Though the ingredient list runs a bit long, I've always found the drink well worth the effort. It has the potency that tiki-style cocktails are known for, and it's pleasantly tart, not too sweet, and nicely layered.

GLASS: Highball	GARNISH: Edible flower

2 oz/60 ml dark rum

1 oz/30 ml 151-proof rum

1 oz/30 ml fresh lime juice

1 oz/30 ml fresh orange juice

½ oz/15 ml passion fruit syrup

½ oz/15 ml falernum syrup (see Tip, page 101)

Splash of Pernod

Splash of Homemade Grenadine (see Tip, page 25)

Dash of Angostura bitters

Edible flower, for garnish

In a cocktail shaker, add the dark rum, 151-proof rum, lime juice, orange juice, passion fruit syrup, falernum syrup, Pernod, grenadine, and bitters. Add ice and shake until chilled. Strain into a cocktail glass over crushed ice. Garnish with an edible flower. Makes 1 cocktail.

About Falernum

Falernum can be found in two forms: as a liqueur or a syrup. Like orgeat, it has a base of almonds, but it is spicier, with layers of ginger and cloves and accented with lime. It is another wonderful ingredient to have on your bar cart if you enjoy tiki-style drinks. My favorite brand of syrup is Tippleman's.

PUKA PUNCH

The original version of this drink is attributed to Ray Buhen of LA's famed Tiki-Ti bar, whose tropical cocktails have long inspired fans to try to recreate them. Though his cocktail recipes are close-held secrets, I hope this version is a valid tribute to Buhen's original.

GLASS: Hurricane or highball	GARNISH: Orange wedge and mint sprig
1 oz/30 ml dark rum 1 oz/30 ml fresh orange juice 1 oz/30 ml pineapple juice ¾ oz/22 ml passion fruit syrup	½ oz/15 ml falernum syrup (see Tip, page 101) Dash of Angostura bitters ¾ oz/22 ml 151-proof rum Orange wedge, for garnish Mint sprig, for garnish

In a cocktail shaker, add the dark rum, orange juice, pineapple juice, passion fruit syrup, falernum, and bitters. Add ice and shake until chilled. Strain into a cocktail glass over ice cubes or crushed ice. Carefully pour the 151-proof rum over the back of a barspoon into the glass so it floats on top. Garnish with an orange wedge and mint sprig. Makes 1 cocktail.

TROPICAL SOUR

Here, the whiskey in a classic whiskey sour is replaced with rum to delightful effect. The cinnamon simple syrup lends just the right dose of tiki-style spice, and the fresh lime provides the requisite sour note.

GLASS: Old fashioned	GARNISH: Cocktail cherry and lime wedge

2 oz/60 ml dark rum

1½ oz/45 ml fresh lime juice

¾ oz/22 ml Cinnamon Simple Syrup (see Tip, page 63)

1 organic egg white*

Cocktail cherry, for garnish

Lime wedge, for garnish

In a cocktail shaker, add the rum, lime juice, simple syrup, and egg white. Shake until frothy. Add ice and shake until chilled. Strain into a cocktail glass over ice and garnish with a cocktail cherry and lime wedge. Makes 1 cocktail.

*If you have health and safety concerns, you may wish to avoid cocktails made with raw eggs.

BARRACUDA

Though featured on Trader Vic's menus, this cocktail appears to have originated on an Italian cruise ship as a marketing vehicle for Galliano liqueur. With its golden color and use of sparkling wine, the Barracuda is on the elegant end of the spectrum for tiki-style drinks.

GLASS: Coupe or flute	GARNISH: Pineapple wedge and mint leaf

2 oz/60 ml pineapple juice

1½ oz/45 ml golden rum

½ oz/15 ml Galliano liqueur

½ oz/15 ml fresh lime juice

1½ oz/45 chilled sparkling white wine

Pineapple wedge, for garnish

Mint leaf, for garnish

In a cocktail shaker, add the pineapple juice, rum, Galliano, and lime juice. Add ice and shake until chilled. Strain into a cocktail glass. Top with the sparkling wine. Garnish with a pineapple wedge and mint leaf. Makes 1 cocktail.

SUFFERING BASTARD

Here's an interesting rum-free tiki-style drink that's easy to make and doesn't require a cabinet full of ingredients. Sources differ as to whether brandy or bourbon should be used, but both are delicious.

GLASS: Highball	GARNISH: Mint sprig

1½ oz/45 ml gin

1½ oz/45 ml brandy or bourbon

½ oz/15 ml fresh lime juice

¼ oz/7 ml Turbinado Syrup (see Tip, page 75)

2 dashes Angostura bitters

4 oz/120 ml chilled ginger beer

Mint sprig, for garnish

In a cocktail glass, add the gin, brandy, lime juice, turbinado syrup, and bitters and stir. Fill the glass with ice and add the ginger beer. Garnish with a mint sprig. Makes 1 cocktail.

TRIUMVIRATE PUNCH

Martin Cate, with his San Francisco bar (and book of the same name), Smuggler's Cove, is one of the newest additions to the tiki-style cocktail brain trust. This recipe is adapted from one of Cate's original creations. While you'll need to visit the bar to enjoy the best version, along with Cate's specially curated rums, you can still approximate the fruity, spicy, and delicious flavors at home.

GLASS: Old fashioned	GARNISH: Freshly grated nutmeg and mint sprig
2 oz/60 light rum	¼ oz/7 ml allspice dram (see Tip, page 129)
2 oz/60 ml passion fruit syrup	2 dashes Angostura bitters
1 oz/30 ml fresh lime juice	Freshly grated nutmeg, for garnish
¼ oz/7 ml Honey Syrup (see page 41)	Mint sprig, for garnish

In a cocktail shaker, add the rum, passion fruit syrup, lime juice, honey syrup, allspice dram, and bitters. Add ice and shake until chilled. Strain into a cocktail glass over crushed ice and garnish with grated nutmeg and a mint sprig. Makes 1 cocktail.

VACATION

BLUE HAWAII

Often confused with the Blue Hawaiian, the Blue Hawaii is an entirely different drink. There's no coconut in this one, and it's as clear as Hawaiian ocean water. But if you have a bottle of blue Curaçao on your liquor shelf, here's another tasty way of using it.

GLASS: Hurricane or highball	GARNISH: Lemon wedge and mint sprig
3 oz/90 ml pineapple juice	½ oz/15 ml fresh lime juice
1 oz/30 ml light rum	½ oz/15 ml fresh lemon juice
1 oz/30 ml vodka	Lemon wedge, for garnish
½ oz/15 ml blue Curaçao	Mint sprig, for garnish
½ oz/15 ml Simple Syrup (see Tip, page 62)	

In a cocktail shaker, add the pineapple juice, rum, vodka, Curaçao, simple syrup, lime juice, and lemon juice. Add ice and shake until chilled. Strain into a cocktail glass over ice and garnish with a lemon wedge and mint sprig. Makes 1 cocktail.

HEMINGWAY DAIQUIRI

This was allegedly Ernest Hemingway's usual drink at his favorite bar in Havana. He had a reputation for drinking many of them per night. Use pink grapefruit juice for an extra-pretty drink. Choose this when you want a tiki-style cocktail that is fruit-forward but not too sweet.

GLASS: Coupe		GARNISH: Lime wheel

2 oz/60 ml light rum

¾ oz/22 ml fresh lime juice

¾ oz/22 ml fresh grapefruit juice

½ oz/15 ml maraschino liqueur

Lime wheel, for garnish

In a cocktail shaker, add the rum, lime juice, grapefruit juice, and maraschino liqueur. Add ice and shake until chilled. Strain into a chilled cocktail glass and garnish with a lime wheel. Makes 1 cocktail.

151 SWIZZLE

A touch of anise from the Pernod and botanicals from the bitters flavor this high-proof rum drink invented by Donn Beach at his namesake bar, Don the Beachcomber, in the 1960s. Don't skip the nutmeg, as it is essential to the full aromatic experience of the cocktail.

GLASS: Old fashioned	GARNISH: Freshly grated nutmeg, cinnamon stick, edible flower, & pineapple fronds

1½ oz/45 ml 151-proof rum	Freshly grated nutmeg, for garnish
½ oz/15 ml Turbinado Syrup (see Tip, page 75)	Cinnamon stick, for garnish
½ oz/15 ml fresh lemon juice	Edible flower, for garnish
Splash of Pernod	Pineapple fronds, for garnish
2 dashes Angostura bitters	

In a cocktail shaker, add the rum, turbinado syrup, lemon juice, Pernod, and bitters. Add ice and shake until chilled. Strain into a cocktail glass over crushed ice and garnish with freshly grated nutmeg, a cinnamon stick, an edible flower, and pineapple fronds. Makes 1 cocktail.

About Bitters

Though not necessarily bitter in flavor, bitters are made by infusing a neutral alcohol base with a proprietary blend of botanicals, herbs, spices, and citrus to create an intense flavoring agent. Think of bitters as the seasoning for your cocktail—as if you were reaching for salt, pepper, or a favorite spice to add punch to your drink. In tiki-style cocktails, Angostura bitters is a preferred brand.

SHARK'S TOOTH

A Trader Vic's invention, the Shark's Tooth amps up the typical pineapple and lime juice components with a touch of cherry liqueur and fruity grenadine. Cut the pineapple garnish into a triangle so it resembles an appropriate tooth.

GLASS: Old fashioned	GARNISH: Cocktail cherry and pineapple wedge
1½ oz/45 ml light rum	½ oz/15 ml maraschino liqueur
1½ oz/45 ml dark rum	½ oz/15 ml Homemade Grenadine (see Tip, page 25)
½ oz/15 ml fresh lime juice	
½ oz/15 ml pineapple juice	Cocktail cherry, for garnish
½ oz/15 ml Simple Syrup (see Tip, page 62)	Pineapple wedge, for garnish

In a cocktail shaker, add the light rum, dark rum, lime juice, pineapple juice, simple syrup, maraschino liqueur, and grenadine. Add ice and shake until chilled. Strain into a cocktail glass over ice and garnish with a cocktail cherry and pineapple wedge. Makes 1 cocktail.

BLACKBEARD'S GHOST

|

This cocktail is credited to Jeff "Beachbum" Berry and is one of the new additions to the tiki-style cocktail canon. This drink has a nice balance of fruit flavors and a blend of rums, with solid underpinnings of spice.

GLASS: Double old fashioned	GARNISH: Citrus boat* and mint sprig
1 oz/30 ml fresh orange juice	½ oz/15 ml fresh lemon juice
1 oz/30 ml light rum	½ oz/15 ml fresh lime juice
½ oz/15 ml dark rum, preferably Demerara	½ oz/15 ml Turbinado Syrup (see Tip, page 75)
½ oz/15 ml apricot liqueur	2 dashes Angostura bitters
½ oz/15 ml falernum syrup (see Tip, page 101)	Citrus boat*, for garnish
	Mint sprig, for garnish

In a cocktail shaker, add the orange juice, light rum, dark rum, apricot liqueur, falernum, lemon juice, lime juice, turbinado syrup, and bitters. Add ice and shake until chilled. Strain into a cocktail glass over ice cubes or crushed ice and garnish with a citrus boat and mint sprig. Makes 1 cocktail.

*To make a citrus boat, affix two wide sections of orange peel to a lime shell with cocktail picks to resemble sails.

RUM BARREL

The ingredient list is long in this Donn Beach classic cocktail, but you'll find it's worth assembling all the pieces. I've designed this one to share with someone special.

GLASS: Tiki mug	GARNISH: Citrus wedges, ti leaf and edible flower
4 oz/120 ml dark rum 2 oz/60 ml *each* fresh grapefruit, lime, orange, and pineapple juices 2 oz/60 ml Honey Syrup (see Tip, page 41) 2 oz/60 ml *each* light rum and golden rum ½ oz/15 ml allspice dram (see Tip, page 129)	¼ oz/7 ml falernum syrup, (see Tip, page 101) Small splash Pernod Small splash Homemade Grenadine (see Tip, page 25) 2 dashes Angostura bitters 2 cups/300 g ice cubes Citrus wedges, for garnish Ti leaf and edible flower, for garnish

In a high-speed blender, combine the dark rum, grapefruit juice, lime juice, orange juice, pineapple juice, honey syrup, light rum, golden rum, allspice dram, falernum, Pernod, grenadine, bitters, and ice cubes. Blend until smooth, then divide between 2 cocktail glasses. Garnish with citrus wedges, a ti leaf, and an edible flower. Makes 2 cocktails.

About Allspice Dram

Also known as pimiento dram, allspice dram is an elixir made from allspice berries that is popular in the West Indies. It is used in many tiki-style drinks as a way to bring a spice component to the mix. Many describe the flavor of allspice as a combination of cinnamon, clove, and nutmeg. My favorite brand is St. Elizabeth.

DR. FUNK

Allegedly one of the earliest tiki-style drinks ever created, this cocktail was inspired by Robert Louis Stevenson's personal doctor. Sources say that the original tonic, later transformed into a cocktail, was developed by the doctor to treat melancholy in his patients. This version is tart and refreshing, shot through with anise flavor, and boasts a pretty orange color.

GLASS: Double old fashioned	GARNISH: Mint sprig

2½ oz/75 ml golden rum	¼ oz/7 ml Pernod
1 oz/30 ml fresh lime juice	Sparkling water
½ oz/15 ml Turbinado Syrup (see Tip, page 75)	Mint sprig, for garnish
¼ oz/7 ml Homemade Grenadine (see Tip, page 25)	

In a cocktail shaker, add the rum, lime juice, turbinado syrup, grenadine, and Pernod. Add ice and shake until chilled. Strain into a cocktail glass over crushed ice and top with sparkling water. Garnish with a mint sprig. Makes 1 cocktail.

WHITE SANDS COFFEE

Here is a tropical take on an Irish coffee for those days when your vacation gets rained out. The coconut whipped cream is also good on fresh berries or whenever you want a vegan alternative to dairy-based whipped cream.

GLASS: Coffee mug	GARNISH: Cinnamon stick and toasted coconut flakes
2 demerara sugar cubes 5 oz/150 ml strong, hot, dark-roast brewed coffee 2 oz/60 ml dark rum 1 oz/30 ml Kahlúa	Coconut Whipped Cream (see Tip, page 135) Cinnamon stick, for garnish Toasted coconut flakes, for garnish

Put the sugar cubes in a preheated mug and fill with coffee. Stir until the sugar is dissolved. Add the rum and Kahlúa and stir briefly. Top with a generous amount of coconut whipped cream and garnish with a cinnamon stick and toasted coconut flakes. Serve warm. Makes 1 cocktail.

Coconut Whipped Cream

Chill 1 can (13.5 oz/380 ml) unsweetened full-fat coconut milk for 24 hours. Using a chilled bowl and whisk attachment on a stand mixer, beat the solid cap of cream on top of the coconut milk (save the liquid for another use) with 2 Tbsp powdered sugar and 1 tsp pure vanilla extract until light and fluffy.

LAGOON SWOON

|

On a recent trip to Tahiti, I found that fresh mango juice was ubiquitous in the restaurants and bars. The memory of that delicious flavor spurred me to create my own tiki-style cocktail. Its name is a nod to the swoon-worthy lagoon that separated the hotel's swimming and snorkeling waters from the open ocean.

GLASS: Old fashioned	GARNISH: Mint sprig and dried citrus wheel

2 oz/60 ml mango juice

2 oz/60 ml coconut rum

½ to ¾ oz/15 to 22 ml Star Anise Simple Syrup (see Tip, page 63), depending on the sweetness of the mango juice

½ oz/15 ml fresh lime juice

Mint sprig, for garnish

Dried citrus wheel, for garnish

In a cocktail shaker, add the mango juice, rum, simple syrup, and lime juice. Add ice and shake until chilled. Strain into a cocktail glass over ice and garnish with a mint sprig. Makes 1 cocktail.

JASPER'S JAMAICAN

This simple drink, which some refer to as a Jamaican-style daiquiri, was created by Jasper LeFranc of the Bay Roc Hotel in Montego Bay in the 1960s. It's a great one to pick when you want the flavor of a tiki-style drink but don't want one with multiple elements. Choose this if you're in the mood for a spice-forward cocktail rather than a sweeter, fruit-forward drink.

GLASS: Coupe	GARNISH: Freshly grated nutmeg and grapefruit twist

1¼ oz/37 ml golden rum, preferably Jamaican

½ oz/15 ml allspice dram (see Tip, page 129)

¼ oz/7 ml fresh lime juice

¼ oz/7 ml Simple Syrup (see Tip, page 62)

Freshly grated nutmeg, for garnish

Grapefruit twist, for garnish

In a cocktail shaker, add the rum, allspice dram, lime juice, and simple syrup. Add ice and shake until chilled. Strain into a cocktail glass and garnish with freshly grated nutmeg and a grapefruit twist. Makes 1 cocktail.

NUI NUI

Donn Beach had another hit on his hand with this spice-forward cocktail that blends two types of rum, two types of citrus juices, and two types of infused syrups. Some cocktail scholars claim it is a perfect Christmas cocktail, evoking the flavors of baking during the winter holidays.

GLASS: Old fashioned	GARNISH: Orange wheel and edible flower

1½ oz/45 ml golden rum

¾ oz/22 ml fresh lime juice

¾ oz/22 ml fresh orange juice

½ oz/15 ml dark rum

½ oz/15 ml Cinnamon Simple Syrup (see Tip, page 63)

½ oz/15 ml Vanilla Simple Syrup (see Tip, page 63)

¼ oz/7 ml allspice dram (see Tip, page 129)

Dash of Angostura bitters

Orange wheel, for garnish

Edible flower, for garnish

In a cocktail shaker, add the golden rum, lime juice, orange juice, dark rum, cinnamon simple syrup, vanilla simple syrup, and allspice dram and bitters. Add ice and shake until chilled. Strain into a cocktail glass over crushed ice and garnish with an orange wheel and edible flower. Makes 1 cocktail.

PONCHE DE CRÈME

The traditional drink of the Christmas season in Trinidad, Ponche de Crème is similar to American eggnog

GLASS: Wineglass	GARNISH: Freshly grated nutmeg, lime twist, and paper umbrella
4 large organic eggs* Finely grated zest of 1 lime 3 cans (each 14 oz/400 g) sweetened condensed milk 1 can (12 oz/355 ml) evaporated milk	12 oz/360 ml golden rum 6 dashes Angostura bitters 1 tsp freshly grated nutmeg, plus more for garnish Lime twist, for garnish Paper umbrella, for garnish

In a large bowl, add the eggs and lime zest. Using an electric mixer, beat the eggs until light and fluffy. While beating, gradually pour in the sweetened condensed milk and evaporated milk until smooth. Stir in the rum and bitters. Strain through a fine-mesh sieve into a large container and stir in the nutmeg. Cover tightly and chill for at least 1 hour or up to overnight. Pour into cocktail glasses and garnish with grated nutmeg, lime twists, and paper umbrellas. Makes 6 to 8 cocktails.

*If you have health and safety concerns, you may wish to avoid cocktails made with raw eggs.

YELLOW BIRD

There seems to be no definitive version of the Yellow Bird, but legend has it that the cocktail originally hails from Jamaica. My version uses Galliano (which adds a spice component) and banana liqueur (which adds a tropical fruit component).

GLASS: Old fashioned		GARNISH: Lime wedge
1 oz/30 ml light rum		¼ oz/7 ml Galliano liqueur
1 oz/30 ml dark rum		¼ oz/7 ml banana liqueur
1 oz/30 ml fresh orange juice		Lime wedge, for garnish
½ oz/15 ml fresh lime juice		

In a cocktail shaker, add the light rum, dark rum, orange juice, lime juice, Galliano, and banana liqueur. Add ice and shake until chilled. Strain into a cocktail glass over crushed ice. Garnish with a lime wedge. Makes 1 cocktail.

RESOURCES

Here are some resources that are useful for finding the ingredients called for in this book and stocking your home tiki lounge.

Total Wine & More

I always advocate for patronizing local businesses, but not every community liquor store will source a full array of rum and other ingredients for tiki-style cocktails. Total Wine & More has a reputation for having an extended array of rum and other spirits for all your tiki-style drink needs.
Totalwine.com

Liquid Alchemist

Premium cocktail syrups for serious cocktail makers. Included in their line are passion fruit, grenadine, orgeat, and falernum as well as other tropical flavors to experiment with. Liquid-alchemist.com

Tippleman's

Maker of craft cocktail syrups, including my favorite falernum. Tipplemans.com

Cocktail Kingdom

A source for bar tools, glassware, and other bar cart needs. Cocktailkingdom.com

INDEX

Index